EIGHT EXTRAORDINARY YEARS

in the LIVES of

FIVE ORDINARY PEOPLE

A Retrospective View

By
Barbara M. Darrell

INFINITY
PUBLISHING

Copyright © 2007 by Barbara M. Darrell

ISBN 0-7414-4015-6

Printed in the United States of America

Published November 2010

INFINITY PUBLISHING
1094 New DeHaven Street, Suite 100
West Conshohocken, PA 19428-2713
Toll-free (877) BUY BOOK
Local Phone (610) 941-9999
Fax (610) 941-9959
Info@buybooksontheweb.com
www.buybooksontheweb.com

This memoir is dedicated to:

My husband, Bernie, and RCA,
who made it happen.

My children, Brenda, Mark, and Carl, who lived it.

My grandchildren, Everett, Elizabeth, and Matthew, whom
I pray will take wings, see the world,
and love and appreciate all its people.

Contents

Foreword

It was certainly not the norm for a black family to travel throughout the United States and to distant, exotic places in the turbulant sixties, during the Civil Rights Movement and preceding the Civil Rights Act. Our parents were adamant about the fact that exposure to different places, people, and cultures was essential to the development of a person. Thus, despite the many obstacles which confronted us — having to consult the Department of Interior about lodging availability, carefully considering routes because of eating and lodging facilities, and mostly avoiding the South for obvious reasons — we traveled. Although many of my parents' friends felt they were incautious in traveling to numerous places throughout the United States, my parents persisted. Travel for me began with a trip to El Paso, Texas, when I was only nine months old.

However much we had traveled earlier, my father's appointment to the small, utopian coral island of Kwajalein was indeed a dream realized for the entire family. In 1966, this beautiful island represented the ideal social, political, educational, and pleasure domes. We engaged in outdoor activities all year: boating, swimming, fishing, golfing, soccer, volleyball, and softball. Yet, on the other hand, our academic and social lives were challenging and fulfilling. There was almost a total absence of prejudice in the schools and in entertainment, since this was a government facility. We played and socialized with everyone. It is difficult to measure how this period of utopian living, where freedom from stress and anxiety were omnipresent, played in our development. Although we were not physically in the United States when Dr. Martin Luther King, Jr., was assassinated and riots erupted in Black communities across the country, spiritually, we felt the pain and the sadness that all Black people suffered.

While living on Kwajalein, we had the unique opportunity for a two-month trip around the world. It was the epicenter of our many travels all over the world, and it was, for my mother and father and for the three of us, the culmination of many dreams to see, to enjoy, and to learn about other cultures and other people. For us, this was a trip of a lifetime, and the memories will always be with us.

A hymn of praise to my Mother for undertaking the arduous task of recapturing our memories of this glorious period in our lives; it will be a lasting legacy for us and our children.

A proud daughter......*Brenda A. Darrell, MD*

Chapter 1

INTRODUCTION

For almost eight years, my family and I lived encapsulated in what we called "our time in paradise." Those extraordinary years were without comparison. Nowhere in our previous lives had we anticipated such enlightenment, such visions. It was a period of grace to which we had vaguely aspired, but had not truly expected.

My husband, an electrical engineering leader at RCA, had heretofore been traveling extensively for his company, while I, the dutiful housewife and doting mother, became the entertainer, cook, and chief bottle-washer, valiantly shuttling our three children to the doctor, football practices, ballet lessons, Girl and Boy Scout meetings, and sundry activities. Although this was expected and I always rose to the occasion, it was not, to be sure, the ideal situation. Every wife wants that close-knit family in which all members of the family eat together every night, or as close to that ideal as possible.

Finally, in one fell swoop, Bernie received the ideal job to which almost everyone aspired, or would have loved: an opportunity for a tour of duty in the Pacific Marshall Islands, on a coral atoll called Kwajalein. Although this job would entail massive upheavals in our family — our children would have to leave their friends and their schools, and for that matter, so would we — the advantages of such a position far outweighed any negative connotations we may have entertained.

For one thing, the island itself was known by all RCA members as a virtual paradise — exciting work, yet beautiful and serene. In addition, a tour there would give one years of tax relief, plus innumerable weeks of accumulated time to do with as one pleased. To say we were elated with this assignment is clearly an understatement; we were delirious with joy, and could hardly wait to begin all the tedious tasks of preparation for the transition to the island. And we were absolutely correct in our anticipated joy. This is our retrospective of eight years in paradise: the things we saw, the places we visited, the people we met, the "around the world" trip we took, the changes to our lives, and the world view that emerged in our visions. It was, to be sure, a life-changing experience that was to last a life time. These were years steeped in peace and tranquility.

Preparations for our departure were numerous. We decided to rent out all but the top floor of our home; school transfers for Brenda and Mark were needed; and immunizations were needed for everyone. Passports were an absolute necessity for all of us, and we eventually found a patient photographer who was able to capture a group passport picture that resembled us.

Family Passport
(Group passport pictures are no longer allowed.)

On Kwajalein, winter and Sunday clothing would not be necessary, and I could not even imagine not shopping for winter or Easter clothing at Jacob Reeds or Best & Co; we had spent a lot of money in those stores over the years. In addition, our departure involved giving away unnecessary items. What to give away and what to keep became a family project: we gave the really good winter clothing to family and friends, and we gave a ton of clothing and toys to charity, although some things we should have kept, like winter coats. And all the beautiful dolls; Brenda just knew she would never play with those dolls again, so to the sidewalk they went. Oh, the dolls — I still remember the line of assorted dolls standing near our curb for some lucky family to acquire. Finally, after weeks of preparation, we were packed and on the island by March of 1966, one week before Brenda's tenth birthday.

Our travels had actually started in 1963, when we decided to take a long family vacation. In the late spring of that year, we traveled cross-country visiting national parks and monuments; our final destination was California, where we would visit with friends. En route, we visited the Grand Canyon in Arizona; Frijoles Canyon in New Mexico; the Black Hills of South Dakota; and San Francisco, California. Because we did not want problems, we had carefully selected all accommodations through the Department of the Interior, staying in national parks and areas surrounding the monuments, plus we used a little book we had found called *A Black Family Travels Coast to Coast.*

On our return trip, we stayed in Yellowstone National Park, Salt Lake City, and Yosemite National Park. Salt Lake City was the only site where our arrangements were not made in advance. Fortunately, when we arrived in Salt Lake City at five o'clock in the morning and randomly selected a motel, a most gracious hosteler, clad in her nightclothes, greeted us with a smile; she responded to our request with adequate accommodations for five weary travelers.

During that month, we learned that we had good little travelers, which was exciting for us because travel was our passion. We now knew that the children could take the constant changes that travel necessitates, and they rather enjoyed the experience. They were observant, interested, and never bored; it was as though they knew they were to absorb every aspect of this venture. Brenda and I discussed the style and décor of hotel/motel rooms and restaurants, to which the boys always added their preferences or dislikes. There were no complaints about the length of the ride, and no whining — not even from little Carl. They loved restaurant eating and

4

sleeping in different hotels, and the cabins were as exciting to them as they were to us.

We long ago realized how much travel broadens one's horizons, and now we could plan to impose our passion on the family. We were interested in seeing the States and as much of the world as possible. At that time, however, we had no idea how much of the world we would see.

Chapter 2

ISLAND of PARADISE

Kwajalein is a small island in the Marshall Islands, 2,163 miles southwest of Honolulu.

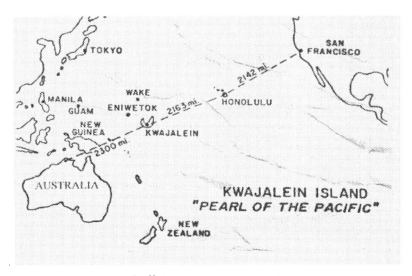

A distance measurement

It is a missile range run by the United States government, and subcontracted by Massachusetts Institute of Technology, Radio Corporation of America, Bell Laboratories, Kentron, and others. From this site, missiles launched from Vandenberg, California, are picked up over the Pacific and tracked until they splash down into the Pacific waters. It is the only facility that allows the United States to track its long-range ballistic missiles throughout their full flights. I suppose its original claim to fame is that it was one of the sites where the Japanese stockpiled ammunition and aircraft to bomb Pearl Harbor. Of course, our participation in World

6

War II was the result of this attack, and more than one hundred and one battles raged until the close of the war.

A re-entry phenomenon

Since there were no jet flights at that time, we had a ten-hour flight from Honolulu to Kwajalein on World Airlines, which had the responsibility of carrying all families and passengers to this secret island. It was ten hours of eating, drinking, and getting acquainted with others who were also going to the island. Finally, we arrived at Kwajalein Airport where the sun was high, hot and blinding. Although my emotions ran the gamut, I was grateful for having completed a long journey safely; I immediately pondered, however, how I would tolerate the intense heat. A sea of smiling faces greeted us, welcoming us to this paradise. Having just come from California and Hawaii, I quickly noticed that the sea of faces seemed pale, but friendly and welcoming nonetheless. I had the highest feeling of elation in anticipation of this new adventure; since it was an assignment we had hoped and dreamed of, we were anticipating new adventures, knowing full well that they would add dimensions to our growth and enlightenment.

This island, Kwajalein, was a coral reef, so there was no fertile soil to promote growth of vegetation and beautiful flowers. Nonetheless, there were palm and breadfruit trees, and a limited assortment of flowers. Hibiscus were among the most flourishing flowers, colorful in their own way in many hues. What Kwajalein lacked in verdant lushness, it made up for in smiling faces, congeniality, friendliness, and its relaxed atmosphere. During this tour, watching these people, I often wished people would get along as well in the States; although some of it may have been superficial, it still felt good to engage in such open friendliness.

On our first night on Kwajalein, we were entertained by the Auchenbachs, our sponsoring family. Undoubtedly because they had no children, they were thrilled to meet ours. Of course, John Auchenbach and Bernie had worked together in the States, so they were not strangers. Actually, Bernie replaced John in the States when John took this temporary assignment on Kwajalein. Moreover, John and Anna were a wonderful couple: John was a quiet, gentle intellect, while Anna was gregarious, fun-loving, a world traveler, and a celebrated portrait painter. Anna's tales of Kwajalein and her world travel held us spellbound until it was time to be shown our new home.

Standard procedure required a sponsoring family to welcome new arrivals and acquaint them with the island and facilities, and John and Anna did their job magnificently. In addition to the usual procedures, they also gave a delightful dinner at their trailer that was relaxed and informative. Afterwards, we were taken to our assigned trailer — number 505.

Here we were, in the heat of the Marshall Islands, on a coral reef, about to call a trailer our home, whereas in Moorestown, we had four bedrooms; Mark and Carl shared a very large bedroom, while Brenda had her own feminine bedroom complete with canopied bed. Our house in the suburbs had two-and-a-half baths and a recreation room for activities extending beyond the bedrooms. Although our three-bedroom trailer on this coral reef had an adequate bedroom for Bernie and me, there was only one bathroom. How ever would we manage?

Moreover, we also exchanged two cars for six bicycles, one of which was needed for parts, because bike rusting was a major problem on the island. We islanders biked everywhere, rain or shine — to school, church, work, the movies, parties — even attired in long muumuus, just everywhere. There was one exception: Bernie flew to work every day, since he worked on the island of Roi-Namur, about forty miles north of Kwajalein. Still, he biked to the airport.

Our home in Moorestown, New Jersey

Our home on Kwajalein: Trailer #505, after the addition of a patio cover. (Our residence spring 1966 – summer 1970)

Chapter 3

HONOLULU, HAWAII

To reach this little paradise, we had had to go through Honolulu, Hawaii. Was that easy or what! We planned to spend several days in Los Angeles sightseeing and visiting friends. When we arrived in Los Angeles, Bernie directed the cab driver to take us to the Bel Air Motel; evidently, the driver did not hear "motel" and took us to the Hotel Bel Air, the deluxe hotel of the rich and famous. As we were driving up the hill to this magnificent, opulent, beautiful hotel, we realized that we had been taken to the wrong location. Enjoying a long, hearty laugh, Bernie corrected the driver, and we shortly arrived at the upscale Bel Air Motel, only to find that we had some businessman's suitcase instead of our own. We knew he would return ours, since it was filled with children's clothing, and he did. After the exchange of suitcases, our holiday began.

Having been to California but never to Honolulu, we had Honolulu on our minds, and were eagerly awaiting our first glimpses of the city. There is something exhilarating about arriving at a territory never before seen. Our steps quickened with great anticipation; the entire family was caught up in the excitement. In those days, we deplaned by walking down the stairs onto the tarmac, where we were met by beautiful, brown Hawaiian girls wearing gloriously colorful muumuus, with huge hibiscuses in their hair in shades of red, yellow, pink, orange, and white. We were introduced to the true island spirit as they placed fragrant leis of plumerias, orchids, hibiscuses, and gardenias around our necks. Indeed, we could smell the fragrance of the flowers and feel the warm trade winds on our faces. Aloha! We were in Hawaii, and what a glorious feeling that was.

One cannot imagine the arrays of beautiful exotic flowers that seemed to be everywhere; they generated in us a lightheaded, happy feeling. Frankly, the vibrantly colored flowers simply staggered the imagination — green, yellow, pink, fuchsia, lavender, orange, and red seemed to be growing everywhere — and the fragrances of these island flowers went straight to the head: the stately birds-of-paradise; the heart-shaped anthurium; the orchids of various hues, some so tiny one could hardly believe they were orchids. Hibiscuses — the largest I have seen anywhere — showed their colors, peeking amid the concrete buildings in every conceivable shade, from the palest to the most vivid.

There were beds of flowers along the streets, and hotel entrances were adorned with the lushness of this tropical paradise. Baskets of flowers seemed to hang from every lamppost and every conceivable place, and — as if these were not enough beauty for us to behold — there, looming in the foreground, was the extinct and majestic volcano, Diamond Head. Although it sat five miles southeast of Honolulu, its silhouette greeted us. We had been in Honolulu all of forty minutes and had already decided that this island had everything!

The taxi driver took five happy people from the airport to the Royal Princess Hotel, where we could see muumuu-clad vendors selling leis. Gigantic modern hotels and both sleek and stately office buildings dotted the landscape. The Aloha Tower, standing tall above the piers where passenger ships dock, seemed to greet us, and the water appeared to wave us an "Aloha!" As our driver took us along the highway, we saw sandy beaches, swaying green palm trees, and several parks where we caught glimpses of basketweaving, hula dancing, and some sports, particularly baseball.

Here was a bustling city, its streets nearly crowded with people of various colors and ethnicities. Most of the people were Hawaiian, of course, but there were many Asians, and we noticed immediately that Caucasians were in the minority here. This was different: it was an island, but we were definitely in a metropolis — one made to attract tourists like us, and we were attracted.

Neither the three-hour time difference nor jet lag affected us; we dropped our bags and headed for Waikiki Beach and the blue Pacific. I was disappointed by the size of Waikiki Beach, since Art Linkletter had convinced me that it was extremely large; however, its beauty was unsurpassed. The sand was golden and gleaming, and contrasted with the azure blue of the water. To stand on the beautiful sands of Waikiki Beach and look across at the bustling city streets was unique and exhilarating to us. I loved the contrast; it pleased me to my soul. Swimming was not on the agenda that day as we had far too much to see.

We followed the sounds of Hawaiian music into the International Market Place; there we found entertainment for the afternoon and evening. Watching the hula dancers, we were intrigued by the ease with which they moved their hips and arms as they swayed to the strumming of the ukulele and the steel drums to tell us an island story. Samoan dancers in grass skirts stepped and swayed with such force that we actually felt the vibrations of the deep drums played by strong, bronzed Samoan drummers.

Meandering, we found and watched wood carvers, basket weavers, and ladies making leis, and we came upon an assortment of Aloha garments. Immediately, we started shopping for Hawaiian shirts for Bernie and the boys, and a red muumuu for Brenda. I chose a turquoise muumuu to match Bernie's shirt. The garments were covered with a hibiscus print, since we had learned that it was the state flower and we were celebrating Hawaii.

Brenda and I were fascinated by the ladies making leis: The flowers were so fragrant and colorful, and the women's fingers so nimble as they strung plumeria, hibiscus, carnations, pikake, gardenias, assorted orchids, and flowers unfamiliar to us into leis for sale, that Brenda and I could not resist purchasing leis and other native artifacts. They displayed artifacts from many South Pacific islands, and some were particularly impressive. For instance, a three-foot-long storyboard from the island of Palau in Micronesia, which had a scene depicting an island story deeply carved into the most beautiful wood, really caught my attention. The board was carved so deeply that the trees and characters stood out from their background dramatically. I was impressed and inquired about the carver, discovering that he was a Palauan named Siik; later we bought a piece of this master carver's work for our home in Moorestown.

Because it was our first night in Hawaii, we wanted to find an unusual restaurant to eat our first meal, and we found one that was elevated and engulfed in Banyan trees. It was extremely beautiful, and had an outside lanai, where we chose to dine. We soon found that pigeons also liked the outer portion of this restaurant. Despite the interruptions, the children were amused and enjoyed ducking the pigeons. Our choice was well founded: the food was absolutely delicious. Bernie and I dined on Mahi Mahi, a delicious fish familiar in Pacific waters, and we were introduced to the Mai Tai, a delicious combination of fruit juices and rum, which became my favorite island drink. Although we urged the children to become adventuresome, they chose what was familiar.

Becoming weary and then extremely exhausted, we decided to bring our first day in Honolulu to a close. Clearly, our first evening in Honolulu was a true departure from our normal life, all of which we thoroughly enjoyed.

The next day we rented a car and drove up the coast to the Polynesian Culture Center, where the true beauty of Oahu could be seen. The vibrant green landscape contrasted with the blue Pacific Ocean, and it was a wondrous sight to behold. Multitudinous trees, shrubs, bushes, and flowers too numerous to mention covered the landscape; it was like a drive-through paradise.

We were absolutely overwhelmed by the beauty. We stopped to absorb the sight of the ocean, all blue-green and golden in the morning sun, we listened to the roar of the ocean as the waves hit the shore with great power then rested on the water's edge, foamy and white. Similarly, we saw blowholes, caves, and enjoyed the beauty of the mountains.

When we reached the Polynesian Culture Center, we toured replicas of villages built by Tahitians (of Tahiti), Samoans (of Samoa), Maori (of New Zealand), Fijians (of Fiji), Tongans (of Tonga), and Polynesians (of Polynesia). Each village's participants were attired in native dress, and some played the music of their cultures. Listening carefully, we were able to distinguish the soft sway of Polynesian music and dance from the more robust steps and resounding beats favored by the Maori. Moreover, the villagers' lives, their dances, and their games were also depicted. I vividly remember the stick game played by the Maori, where bamboo sticks are transferred from one to another at a rapid pace without dropping a stick. It was a game that required dexterity. All of the acts were fun, realistic, and enlightening, and were performed in a fantastic setting.

The next day we took a tour of the Punch Bowl Cemetery and the *USS Arizona* Memorial at Pearl Harbor. The memories awakened were sobering and thought-provoking. History was before all of our eyes: for Bernie and me, it was a reminiscence about that day — December, 7, 1941 — and what we were doing when we heard the dreadful news.

Since our time in Oahu was growing shorter and there were several other sights we wanted to visit, we decided on the Aviary, with its beautifully colored birds of the South Pacific, such as cockatoos, macaw and coral pink flamingos.

Then we ventured on to Sea Life Park to see the variety of marine life. What wonders of nature we enjoyed.

One of the most interesting cultural aspects of Hawaii is the *luau*. Thus, as the sun was setting and the palms were swaying, with the blue Pacific at our backs, we enjoyed our first luau — and what an experience! There were several foods presented to us, but a large pig was the star of the occasion. The smell of roasting pig permeated the air and our nostrils. The pig had been wrapped in *ti* leaves, placed in a pit called an *imu*, and roasted for hours.

The feasting table was covered with coarsely woven brown-and-white *tapa* cloth, and was decorated beautifully with whole pineapples and assorted fruits, such as guavas and mangos, tropical flowers, and *ti* leaves. Some of the foods I remember were *lomi* tuna — a dish of fresh tuna and diced tomatoes — a mixture of chicken and spinach rolled up and steamed, rice, and sundry other foods. Needless to say, the dishes were very tasty, but *poi*, the Hawaiian staple made from taro root, was less appealing.

In addition to food, our luau drink was the Mai Tai, while the children consumed limitless soft drinks. While we dined, we were entertained by Hawaiian music and beautiful hula dancers. As night fell, we were engulfed in island enchantment: tiki torches flickered along the beach, and the city lights from hotels and office buildings created an ambience so beautiful and peaceful that we were filled with pure contentment and joy, resulting in an evening we would never forget.

We knew that we would return in six months, so our hearts were happy and joyful, for we knew this was going to be the adventure of our lives. In six months, there would be another opportunity to see more of this paradise and hear Don Ho sing, "Tiny Bubbles" and "The Hawaiian Wedding Song." Don Ho and his music had quickly become a part of our lives, and we knew this was going to be a great place for rest, relaxation, and shopping. Not only was the Ala Moana Shopping Center the greatest center of its kind in the world, it also had a bonus on the lower level of the center: the best fast-food Chinese restaurant anywhere. It was exceptional and became a must for us on each trip to Honolulu. That evening, our family retired happy, tired and joyful, anticipating the days ahead.

Chapter 4

OUR TRAILER and the

MARSHALLESE PEOPLE

Our home on Kwajalein was a silver trailer; although it was much smaller than our home in Moorestown, it did work well. Brenda, Mark, and Carl absolutely loved it!! Mark and Carl were able to have a long sought-after wish — bunk beds. Brenda had a bedroom so narrow that it was difficult or almost impossible to lie horizontally without her feet touching the wall. She was thrilled. Needless to say, it was different; our bedroom, however, as well as the living and dining room were adequate. Trailer #505 was in a great location — just off a lagoon, which at noon sparkled like a million diamonds dancing in the midday sun. Could anyone ask for more? We could not.

Aside from this beauty, we had the unique opportunity to watch the Marshallese people arrive daily on the *Tarlang*, a troop transport relic from World War II. The Marshallese took the approximately thirty-minute boat ride from their island of Ebeye (north of Kwajalein) each day, arriving about eight o'clock each morning to work in many capacities on Kwajalein. They were primarily laborers, gardeners, and domestics. Although the island of Kwajalein had once belonged to the Marshallese, they were no longer permitted to spend a night on the island. Kwajalein is a part of the Trust Territory of the Pacific Islands, and the United States is its administrator under a trusteeship with the United Nations. Thus, the United States still operates a security base there, and that base provides jobs for the locals, creating an influx of outer islanders. Because of this influx of outer islanders seeking employment on Kwajalein, the island of Ebeye become an overcrowded slum, with poor housing, poor water supply, and nonexistent roads — all of this at the expense of a once proud and beautiful people.

The *Tarlang*, a World War II transport relic

Marshallese women arriving to work on the *Tarlang*

Nevertheless, the Marshallese are an interesting, undaunted, proud group of people. When they arrived daily, they would be conversing with each other, laughing and smiling with a genuine aura of friendliness. Swaying as they walked, they arrived either barefooted or wearing thongs, usually in handmade dresses with loose-fitting bodices and full, gathered skirts in bright colors — reds, blues, oranges, turquoise, and bold prints, vivid enough to brighten the dullest day. Mostly the ladies' dresses were long, below the knee; no shorts or slacks were allowed in this culture. These long, full skirts were necessary so that when the females were seated — and they were almost always seated on the floor, with their legs crossed under them — the dresses completely covered their legs.

Many women worked as domestics, and when they arrived at your home, they left their thongs at the door, as they worked in bare feet. When I arrived on the island, two-dollars-and fifty-cents a day was the going rate for their service, and this was an inflated price. At that price, help was available to anyone who wanted it. Although these women were not usually status seekers, as in most cultures, they learned status from us. Consequently, each woman tried to work for the big man in the big house, and thus, those in trailers were the least desirable employers, although almost every American woman on Kwajalein had some sort of service.

The Marshallese, who are Micronesians, are a remarkably gentle people with bright, warm, friendly eyes. They are a kind, loving people with a beautiful spirit. They are always patient, cheerful, and extremely friendly. This was particularly true of the women, who are — like many American women — the nurturers, while their husbands are the breadwinners.

The beauty of these women began with their long, black, shiny tresses, which they groomed with a natural coconut oil, made from coconut palms, and pulled back in shell combs or ribbon. When showers were not available, the women as well as the men and children bathed in the ocean. The women loved perfume, and kept their bodies fragrantly perfumed and oiled. They were, to be sure, darker than their Polynesian cousins, but altogether beautiful in body as well as in spirit. Never once did I witness anger or any displays of ill-temper, as though their greeting *"Yokwe yok,"* which means "love to you," was indeed imbedded in their psyche.

Nevertheless, they do know how to vent their displeasure. I will never forget the aghast expression that came over my longtime friend and maid Maria's face as she watched me count my silver, as I always do, after hosting a very large luncheon or dinner. This time Maria was present, and the simple procedure produced an enormously embarrassing situation for me. Maria somehow thought I was accusing her of stealing; I tried to appease her, but I was horrified myself that I had been so insensitive. I told her repeatedly that this was a custom after a large party; I was most definitely not accusing her of stealing, nor did I in any way remotely think that she had stolen. She merely looked.

You can imagine what happened. After Maria left that day, I never saw her again. Clearly, a lack of communication and a strange cultural difference had resulted in this weird twist of events. No apology on my part had been accepted, yet that quiet sense of dignity and poise had remained an essential part of Maria's character. We were most fortunate and more than happy to have such genial people working for us. Frankly, both the women and their employers benefited from these arrangements; we, because we could certainly use the help, and they, because even those small salaries increased their living standards.

Indeed, we found the Marshallese to be a very sociable people, and family is the center of their lives. They are a gracious people, but do not shake hands when they greet. Instead, they more or less greet with a nod of acknowledgment. Moreover, we could learn something from their beautiful manners, and we could learn from their book of etiquette. While we constantly interrupt each other, they never interrupt two people conversing, nor would they walk between a couple; instead, they would walk around. Such etiquette and exceedingly good manners could be emulated with great success in all cultures.

The Marshallese are most hospitable in their homes, they give children and visitors the highest priority. Additionally, the elders are revered and are given the utmost respect. Rarely do they hurry; to be on time for appointments is not a necessary part of life. In today's vernacular, they appear to be laid back. However, some of the women, as in other cultures, must work.

Another way in which their culture somewhat differs from ours is within the home. Our homes are almost always devoted to one family unit — father, mother, and children — whereas in their culture, large extended families live together, not only with father, mother, and children, but also with many other relatives and grandparents. This resulted in a very sociable, caring people, who helped each other as well as other people.

Religion for the Marshallese was also varied: there were Christians – Protestants and Catholics, along with a few Seventh Day Adventists and Mormons. Although they all are worshipers, the women are the major weekly churchgoers and supporters of the church. Religion is not only important to their spirituality, but also helps to establish their social lives.

Chapter 5

FAMILY ADAPTS to ISLAND LIFE

Because Kwajalein was a small island and really a large neighborhood, the American children had fewer restrictions and boundries than they had in the States. They loved the freedom.

Mark, in particular, was overwhelmed by the freedom and the casual, cavalier approach in the Kwajalein schools. He had come from a Catholic school where classes were larger and more restricted. The first day after school, he came home, bursting through the door, stating, "Mom, you don't even have to raise your hand to go to the bathroom here!" The schools were an immediate hit.

We were introduced to a new people and a new culture. Breadfruit, palm fronds, coral reefs, shelling and sea shells, Japanese glass fishing floats — all became a part of our vocabulary. In his spare time, Bernie played handball, studied, and learned to sail. Brenda took hula lessons and played softball, while Mark stayed on the golf course when he was not learning karate and Carl developed a love for soccer and tee ball.

Brenda and Mark had made friends on the plane and made new friends at school, but Carl was my shadow for four or five weeks. After he became comfortable, he rode his banana-seated bike all over the island; we were forever looking for him. We enrolled him in a nursery school, and I became acquainted with the women's groups, sharpened up my bridge game, and tried to learn more about the Marshallese people. The Darrells settled in nicely to island life. Everyone was exuberant over the new environs; we were learning a great deal about the island, its people, its culture, and enjoying these new experiences and the new interesting style of life.

I will never forget my first Easter on Kwajalein. I was the only member of our family to attend a Protestant sunrise service conducted by Reverend Eldon Buck, pastor of the Methodist chapel on Kwajalein. The celebration was a spectacular outdoor sunrise service to witness the rising of the sun. On the highest point of the island, there was a grass-covered mound, on which stood a single large white wooden cross. With the ocean in the background, one could only hear the roaring ocean and see the white foam as the waves broke on shore.

Suddenly, there was a streak over the horizon that went from a blackish gray to a golden orange glow, widening until the full sun was exposed as the deepest golden-red ball imaginable. Reverend Buck's robe flapped in the breeze as he read and told us the story of the risen Christ. To add to this, because of the International Dateline, we on Kwajalein were the last people on earth to celebrate this Easter morning. To think: the whole world had celebrated Easter, and we brought it to a close. I never once thought about Easter finery for that day; instead, Christ was the focal point. Later that morning, we attended Easter mass as a family. In the afternoon, there was an island Easter egg hunt for the smaller children, which Carl enjoyed. It was a beautiful, spiritual day, one that I will never forget.

Unlike the seasons at home, on Kwajalein the rainy season was hard to adjust to — this was serious rain. All of us wore slickers, not raincoats. A friend called to see how I was adjusting, and I responded that I was waiting for the rain to stop so I could go to the store. She stopped laughing long enough to tell me that if I wanted something from the store, I had better put on my slicker, mount my bike, and get going. That was exactly what I did. Before long, I was actually going to the outdoor movie in the rain. I remember standing in the rain, leaning against a tree, totally relaxed and enjoying the movie. It is amazing how I adjusted!

Needless to say, the rain wreaked havoc with my hair; however, common sense told me to take wigs, so I had gone wig shopping before we departed. Obviously, I was not sure the island beauty shop could handle my hair, and of course, I was correct, but I was ready. Between perms, relaxers, and wigs, we made it through the Pacific and eventually around the world. The natural hair look for blacks came too late for us. Fortunately, we found beauty shops in Honolulu that could accommodate us, and on R&R trips or dental/medical trips, we always included beauty shop appointments. A black beautician at the Regency Hotel was our first hair savior. When he decided to relocate, he gave us the name of another black beautician on Queen Street in Honolulu. She was excellent with perms, and she became a part of our "must do" list on each trip to Honolulu.

Chapter 6

SHOPPING and DINING

on KWAJALEIN

Shopping on Kwajalein was different from the shopping center in Honolulu. Here was a truly one-of-a-kind store, affectionately called "Macy's." Clothing for the entire family was sold in different sections of the store. I called it the one-room department store, featuring various items of clothing for men, women, and children. Jewelry, including Mikimoto pearls and Rolex watches, and Waterford crystal were in full view and sold at military prices. Imagine.

There was nothing like a Macy's special, and when that special was on muumuus and advertised in the *Hourglass*, the local newspaper, excitement was generated on the island. "Attention Wahinis!" would catch every woman's eye; *Wahini* is the Hawaiian lexicon for women. These ads incited women to head for the Macy's porch to stand in line for the big sale. Newcomers are called *Malahinis* and were invited to purchase their first "island formal," while *Kamaainas*, the oldtimers, were asked to purchase muumuus to freshen up their wardrobes. With all categories taken care of, the rush was on.

Another big special might be Monkey Pod: wooden products from the Philippines, such as salad bowl sets, punch bowls, and serving trays. Because these products were unusual and somewhat rare, Monkey Pod drew lots of attention and the longest lines on Macy's porch. Before the doors opened, women waited in line, attempting to be first in the store to peruse the new inventory. I saw a woman with her arms so full of Monkey Pod that another woman actually took an item from the top of her pile, and she could do nothing about it.

I laughed at this craziness and all the other scenes of shopping absurdity. There were many amusing sights. Nevertheless, I got my share of the wooden products. Talk about over-indulging! I just over-bought the stuff. Years later, when I returned home, I tried to sell some, but ended up giving most of it away. I had never thought about the fact that the dishes could not go in the dishwasher.

Although Kwajalein was a very warm island, there was even a fur sale that drew crowds, especially among those women soon returning to the States, where these items could be used. Another great feature of Macy's was its Special Order desk. Here one could order items not regularly stocked, and Macy's would have them shipped in for you. Splendid! Splendid! I ordered my sterling silver and china from the Special Order desk; it was a convenient, easy way to shop, and the products arrived in perfect shape.

In addition, Macy's had an annex affectionately called "Gimbels," which carried small appliances such as rice cookers, air conditioners, inexpensive glasses, dishes, and sundry other things. The annex was a necessary store, but was not nearly as popular as Macy's, the primary store. These stores were so named to replicate the New York Department store rivalries, Macy and Gimbles. Another shopping opportunity on Kwajalein was through a woman with lots of initiative, who had made a Taiwanese connection and took orders for furniture. I got my share: a carved coffee table, a four-seasons screen, a carved secretary, and a set of cedar chests. Only on Kwajalein could an operation like this take place.

In addition to Macy's and Gimbels, another shopping experience was the Micronesian Handicraft Shop located at the airport. There, women volunteered to order, manage, and keep the shop stocked with beautiful Micronesian artifacts. The shop carried hand-carved storyboards from Palau; stick charts, once used to chart the water currents; and Kili bags, which were beautiful pocketbooks hand woven from pandanus leaves.

Other islands were also represented in the shop: from the island of Truk came Trukese devil masks, which were white outlined in black. Tortoise shell jewelry came from Ponape, including narrow and wide bracelets, rings, and rectangular hair pieces; often, these were inlaid with a silver metal. Black coral jewelry was also very much in demand, as well as hair pieces made of mother-of-pearl clamshells. Necklaces made of native shells, seeds, and nuts were also sold, along with a wealth of other desirables.

Despite all the wonderful arts and crafts in the handicraft shop, the only food store, Surfway (the Commissary, in military terminology), was the most important store. I remember the first time I entered Surfway and saw grits and ham hocks; I love grits, but laughed and thought, "Surely they did not import these just for me." At the time, I was unaware of all the Southerners on the island. There were frequent shortages in store supplies; I felt they did well, however, considering everything had to be flown or shipped in.

Furthermore, at least for our family, learning to drink powered or canned milk was tough. When milk did arrive, it was frozen and had to be thawed. I don't think any of us lost weight because of a lack of food; In fact, we ate more filet mignon and lobster than we did in the states. When doing weekly food shopping, our practice was to take a taxi to Surfway and another to return home; the driver would carry the packages into the house, a service that was provided at no cost to island residents. Tipping was not allowed — imagine that.

From shopping to things around the house, any woman's dream was the Trouble Desk. As the name implies, when something broke down in the trailer/house, one simply called the desk and someone arrived as soon as possible to correct the situation, no "Honey, please . . . " necessary. In addition, furniture was also received, exchanged, repaired, and replaced through the Trouble Desk. That was another reason I enjoyed the island so immensely.

While there were several restaurants on the island for our dining pleasure, the Yokwe Yuk Club (officially, the Officers Club) was the more formal dining room. Their special was Thursday steak night — which was "all you can eat" until one young man abused the privilege; then we were limited to one steak per person. That was sufficient as far as I was concerned. Plus, our favorite Sunday brunch was at the Yuk, which consisted of eggs or omelets to order, bacon, ham, sausages, potatoes, assorted fruits, juices, assorted cold meats, a variety of salads, and meats such as beef or pork sliced on request. It was wonderful to dine so sufficiently after Sunday mass, then go home, relax, and enjoy the balance of your day.

Indeed, all the restaurants had excellent chefs, but none had lobster as succulent or an ocean view as magnificent as the Crossroads. Situated right on the ocean, it was a pleasure just to sit, eat, and watch the movement of the water. The Crossroads' lobster was the best served anywhere, on island or off; so memorable was the experience that I can almost place myself in the Crossroads and taste the lobster now. The Crossroads only required casual dress, and was my favorite place for a Friday evening.

The Pacific Dining Room was primarily for bachelors, but everyone was welcome; fried shrimp was their special on Friday nights. The Snack Bar was the favorite hangout of the young people because it was a place to get a quick hamburger and fries. Mostly, the children frequented the

Snack Bar on Friday evenings before going to the movies: it was a good place to have a quick lunch or dinner with your children.

Chapter 8

CTIVITIES and LIVING

ept us busy on Kwajalein, and entertaining omponent. Fortunately, I was raised by a lieved in beautiful table settings and careful ns. On Kwajalein, dining became an art form rtainment. If one accepted an invitation, an owed. It was fun and my recipe collection

it entertainment I enjoyed putting on for the urday afternoon was a "Come as You Are" l a finger food menu — which we called *puu* an — and then called all the ladies about an d and requested that they come to my trailer ressed. Everyone came except one lady who oking. We had such a wonderful afternoon — nuch fun — while our husbands worked.

n the island gave some outstanding dinner of them were great cooks and bakers. We still ven today; in fact, there are several Kwajalein ating around being used currently. I think my g dinner parties and luncheons evolved from

o the entertaining, other great activities nd living was amazing, nothing tedious or t this existence. One example of this was the ld annually, where Dally Field was converted with a ferris wheel, merry-go-round, airplane e Mermaid booth, the Nerve Game, Bingo, a n Toss, and much, much more.

Chapter 7

FRIENDS and FEELINGS

Amazingly, my new friends on Kwajalein lived very near me in New Jersey. Our husbands worked together at RCA; however, I had no true relationships with the wives until we were six thousand miles from home. Since co-workers on a small island must be nice, we encountered no hardships or difficulties. If our new friends had an agenda, certainly this was no place to display it. We were well received and the RCA wives continue to be friends to this day; the couples have dinner every two months, and many of the wives have lunch on an almost weekly basis. Consequently, our friendships have deepened, from sharing the joys of weddings, births, bar mitzvahs, and anniversaries to sympathizing and grieving when there is an illness or loss of family members.

However, RCA wives were not my only island friends. I had friendships with non-RCA wives, black women who remain connected until this day. Although distance prevents frequent visits, we manage to keep in touch; the bond of friendship is strong and permanent. Addie Johnson, an MIT wife, and Barbara Lyght, a military wife, both arrived on the island after my arrival; they became my connection to my race, and only we could share the frustration and hilarity black women face with their hair especially, in a white world. Interestingly enough, we each chose to handle "the hair situation" differently: Barbara chose to relax her hair and then go to the beauty salon for a wash and set; Addie preferred to complete her entire process herself; I resorted to perms in Honolulu and my assortment of wigs when the perms grew out. Technology has relieved black women of this problem, thank God.

Notwithstanding all these good relationships, one afternoon I heard the paperboy berate my son Mark using the N-word. I jumped up from my nap and ran to the door to see what was taking place. I immediately called the *Hourglass* and told the manager I did not want that boy delivering my paper again. He was fired; his father called me that evening to tell me of the number of Negro friends he had. I did not want his friendship, just his respect. Obviously, his mistake was in not teaching his youngster to respect all people.

Kwajalein life was a unique experience in numerous ways, and only one who has lived there can truly relate to those experiences. Since Kwajalein was a military installation, there was a diverse population from almost every region of the United States on the island, plus people from the Philippines and the Marshalls. Frankly, I had never lived so closely with so many different nationalities before, at least not close enough to become friends, entertain them in my home, and become totally involved in their lives. Basically, the care and love of family was the same, while the foods and religions were different because of different ethnic or geographic backgrounds. Kwajalein represented a multi-ethnic and multi-racial mix that was both interesting and educational.

In our mobile U.S. society, many corporations send employees to various parts of the world to perform given tasks, and that is their main focus — to successfully perform the task. I had never lived so close to so many white Southerners before, and it was good to dispel some of the false beliefs I held. Much to my amazement, most of them were very nice people; even though I realized some were only superficially nice, that is true of populations everywhere.

Since I had been educated in integrated schools and worked with people of many various nationalities, I had learned to get along well with most people, despite their regional,

religious, or ethnic differ[...] a lifetime of discriminati[...] if a new acquaintance is [...] Northern or Southern. [...] determine if a person is [...] innuendos, to be sure, bu[...] ignore. The daily injusti[...] me to live anywhere wi[...] Kwajalein was a Utopi[...] States. Bernie and I were [...] children to be the sam[...] fairness.

Many thing[...] was a maj[...] mother who[...] food present[...] as well as [...] invitation w[...] grew.

One really [...] ladies on a [...] party. I plan[...] *puus* in Haw[...] hour beforeh[...] as they were[...] thought I wa[...] so relaxed, s[...]

The women [...] parties; man[...] share recipes[...] cookbooks f[...] love for hos[...] this experien[...]

In addition [...] abounded. I[...] mundane ab[...] full carnival [...] into a midwa[...] ride, Dunk t[...] Fish Pond, C[...]

Barbara at the Kwajalein Carnival, May 28–30, 1966

Our first experience of the carnival was May 28–30, 1966, and what an exciting three days those were! A Carnival Queen would also be selected, so several teenage girls vied for the crown and we each bought chances for our favorite contestant; the crowning took place toward the end of the three-day event. There were twenty-five island organizations sponsoring thirty or more concession stands. Stuffed animals were imported as prizes for the toss and throw games and other games of chance. In addition, there were booths with all kinds of good food and drink, plus cotton candy, snow cones, ice cream, hamburgers, chicken, and ribs — every food one desired to eat out-of-doors was available.

There were go-cart races, and Father Hackett's band from the Assumption School on the island of Majuro was flown in to add to the festivities. The band was composed of Micronesian youth who lived on the island of Majuro; it was a thrill for them to visit Kwajalein, and we were equally pleased to have them and enjoyed the gaiety they generated. The band members were dressed in matching red shirts and khaki trousers with navy stripes down each side, and they marched wearing thongs on their feet.

Moreover, a nightclub was set up called "Duke Kahanamoku's Shack", where Hawaiian musicians, "The Surfers", gave scheduled performances. Further, the school children were also involved with a carnival poster contest, and our Brenda was a winner for the third-and-fourth-grade entries. Not just the islanders, but also the newcomers joined in to contribute to the success of the carnival event. As I looked over the midway, I actually forgot that I was on a three and-a-half square-mile island; the community had arranged such an amazing fete that it was almost unbelievable. Most importantly, the proceeds from those three days supported the Recreation Department.

Another aspect of the island life was the Community Theatre, which gave an annual "Off Broadway" production. *Absence of a Cello* was the first performance for us, and it was quite well done. Similarly, an annual costume party held by PRESS (Pacific Range Experiments for Signature Studies) generated island-wide excitement.

PRESS' "South of the Border Party" First Prize Winner

I remember two of the party themes, primarily because we won first and second prize. The first was "South of the Border," for which Bernie dressed in a tight black toreador outfit with a sombrero, and I wore a long Mexican peasant skirt with peasant blouse and sombrero. I must admit, our costumes were outstanding, and we won first prize. The other party was "A Space Odyssey," where I was Venus, and Bernie, Mars. We won second prize for the silver costumes that I made, having purchased the elaborate fabric while in Honolulu. What fun!!

Other activities abounded: there were many dances featuring "The Young Hawaiians," a group of talented young men who, fortunately, played for most of the island dances. That was truly a great band; their signature song was "Proud Mary," and when I hear that song today, I am transported back to an island dance.

Sailing races and deep sea fishing trips were all a part of the recreational offerings, as well as golf. Although Bernie had no previous experience golfing, he decided that this might be the appropriate time to learn this intricate game. As with most golfers, he learned the basics, but never mastered the game — at least I say that. Sailing was another sport that Bernie enjoyed, and he spent a considerable amount of time sailing.

Handball, a beloved sport carried over from Bernie's childhood, was resumed while on the island and still found to be enjoyable and challenging. It was amazing how many handball players there were on this small speck in the Marshall Islands; Bernie had several formidable opponents, Major William Lyght and Colonel Floyd Johnson were two of them.

Similarly, Bingo was held every Tuesday night at the Officers' Club, and I was a regular whenever possible. We learned to bowl as a family and became league members; however, the children were better bowlers and in a league of their own. Water skiing was another sport learned and enjoyed by Bernie, Mark, and Brenda.

Activities were limitless, and creative people innumerable; Kwajalein was indeed easy to enjoy and love. However, Kwajalein life was not all playtime and parties. The men there were doing very complicated, serious missions in the Pacific arena. Tracking missions was one part of the job, and collecting data and getting it back to Massachusetts Institute of Technology was the important part. Many hours of work went into these processes. Often, parties were cancelled or rescheduled because of special alerts. Because of that, the men and women had to remain flexible and remember the real reason we were there. Because the missions had top priority in our lives, Bernie and others sometimes worked seven days a week, and frequently through the night.

Carl missed his father most when there were night missions and he didn't see his Dad at all. At one period, after thirty days of seven-day work weeks, I was completely exhausted. Remembering Bernie's previous job assignments and aware of my state of mind, a friend suggested I go out on a deep sea fishing trip that some of the ladies had planned; she offered to care for my children. She insisted that the change would give me a lift. Although fishing is not my sport, for a day away, I accepted her offer. Well, that was my first and last deep sea fishing trip.

It had a beautiful start: an azure blue sky, crystal clear water, friendly people, a day heaven sent. When we arrived a great distance out in the ocean, I began to feel nauseous. As the nauseousness increased, my head began to ache and I could hardly stand. I was s-e-a-s-i-c-k, and the day had just begun — so sick, in fact, that I actually prayed to die.

Someone suggested that I go below and lie down, and I staggered down the steps only to be met by the odious smell of gas fumes. The gas fumes and the movement of the boat created for me the worst kind of feeling, one I would not want to experience again. My stomach churned with the movement of the water and my head was spinning like a top out of control. I was pathetically seasick; thus, I was not interested in the number of fish caught nor who caught them. I just wanted off the boat.

When we finally returned to the shore, I called my friend and thanked her for allowing me a day minus the children. But please, I said, no more deep sea fishing; the children were so much kinder to me than the sea.

Many other wonderful events occurred on the island, but one of the most memorable was our son, Mark's birthday. Mark celebrated his ninth birthday on Kwajalein in the month of November, and what was available to us to celebrate was significant. We were able to request a bus to take all of Mark's classmates and his golfing and karate friends to Bachelor's Beach for a cookout and ball games. Although Mark dearly loves the out-of-doors, he had never been able to have an out-of-doors party, and a November beach party could not have happened in New Jersey!

The children played touch football, badminton, volleyball, and some games I think they made up. We had lots of food and soda, and a fantastic birthday cake created by the Pacific Bakery. Mark was a beaming nine-year old when he cut that cake and opened his birthday gift — a set of golf clubs. He was a happy little islander. The party was a huge success, loads of fun for everyone, and a birthday celebration that Mark never forgot. Good old Kwajalein!!

Chapter 9

ISLAND CHRISTMAS

Because Christmas is my favorite season, I wondered just how different Christmas would be in the Marshall Islands: that would be my challenge. Would I be able to create a spiritual, meaningful holiday amid the hot weather, palm trees, and blue Pacific? I love the season with a passion. I love the shopping, the decorating, the food preparation, family and friends, the music, and last, but not least, the true reason for the season. Thus, my first Christmas shopping on the island was strange.

It was hard to adjust to "Sleigh Bells" being played in the air-conditioned Macy's, then walking out to a blast of hot air in my face. However, my first challenge was to secure a live Christmas tree for our family, and although I was in line for the first shipment of fresh Christmas trees, they ran out before I could get one. I decided not to wait for the second shipment and ordered an artificial, flocked tree from Sears, a wonderful buy, since that tree was used for the duration of our stay on the island.

At home in Moorestown, we always had a real flocked tree, and this was the nearest we came to duplicating our previous Christmases. Ornaments were not a problem, as the Macy's Annex had an assortment, and we had shipped some of our favorite decorations for our home and our tree. Soon, the trailer began to take on the look of Christmas, and the Christmas spirit indeed was alive in the Marshall Islands.

Shopping is something I love to do, so I found it a pleasure and a challenge to shop for gifts for the family back in the States. First, gifts had to be purchased early in order to be shipped in time for the holiday; however, the pleasure came in the accessibility of gifts at our disposal that we ordinarily would not have been able to afford. What a pleasure to send my sister a set of china that she really wanted; a Waterford vase for my mother; Monkey Pod pieces — salad bowl sets, Lazy Suzans, and large wooden spoon-and-fork decorative pieces for the kitchen wall, all imports from the Philippines — to neighbors and friends. I could almost anticipate their happiness when they opened the unusual gifts from the islands.

Dinner was another challenge, and I was adamant that I would cook our traditional dinner: turkey, beef, yams topped with marshmallows, greens, and string beans. I also baked my usual cookies, and my friend, Pauline Clark, gave me the recipe for a delicious fruitcake, the first delicious one I ever baked or ate. Needless to say, it was heavenly, filled with lots of pecans purchased in Honolulu and other nuts and fruits purchased at the Commissary.

Nonetheless, as much as we loved the island, we missed our families and friends, but we had much to occupy us. The children received many gifts from Santa, family, and friends, and they were as excited as ever. My sister, her usual thoughtful self, sent books by black authors and books about black people, ones we had requested to keep our children's identity intact.

After opening gifts and eating breakfast, we went to mass and gave thanks for all our blessings. After dinner, Bernie went sailing, a beautiful, unusual sight for a Christmas Day. It was a holiday filled with all the good feelings and warm emotions that we usually feel on Christmas Day; it was beautiful, beautiful! However, Christmas in the heat of the blue Pacific was still hard for me to absorb. During my entire stay, I had difficulty accepting air-conditioned interiors and hot exteriors, and the total absence of seasons.

One of the highlights of the holiday season was to accept the Marshallese invitation to their Christmas celebration on Ebeye. We took the *Tarlang* to Ebeye, along with many other families, to witness the celebration. After spending months selecting colors and fabrics for each church choir and for each of their performances, plus making costumes and uniforms and practicing songs and dances for the festivities, the Marshallese were ready. From the moment we entered the church, each of us felt the love, joy, and spirit of the occasion for which we were assembled. They possess such a warm way of making you feel welcome that their humble surroundings were immediately forgotten, and you are filled with their love, you are transformed.

Not only did the Marshallese have a large live nativity scene portrayed with animals and a most beautiful baby, they also had several choirs taking turns serenading us with their Christmas music. Each choir member was dressed alike in her respective colors, and each had a turn to sing. One cannot imagine how different Marshallese singing is from ours: the Marshallese sing in high-pitched tones with sort of a tinny sound.

After the choirs' singing, the audience was sprayed with perfume by the minister as he walked up and down the aisles: a custom that was never clarified to me, but impressed me nonetheless. It was a heart-warming experience. Before departing, we were each given pieces of candy and enjoyed fellowship with our hosts. The spirit of the holiday was shared by all who attended. Their generosity and beautiful spirit overwhelmed us; it was truly an experience like no other in which we had participated. At our own service at home, we would have each embraced a congregant near us and wished him a happy holiday. With spiritually happy hearts, we returned to Kwajalein glowing in the knowledge that we had shared and enjoyed another culture.

After our first Christmas, with the beauty and the generosity of spirit exhibited by the Marshallese people, I decided that I wanted to give something of myself to these people. Thus, when volunteers were needed to participate in organizing a program to teach the Marshallese children on the island of Ebeye, I gladly offered my services. Clearly, my early childhood credits and my enthusiasm were ample experience for this program. Consequently, we began by clearing out a building similar to a quonset hut and establishing classrooms.

This is what I had imagined the Peace Corps was like, and I jumped to the challenge with gusto. Although I have forgotten the name of the person in charge, I do remember that directions and approval of volunteers came from Saipan, the seat of government for the Marshalls. After the classrooms were set up, we started to register children.

This schooling was to be for kindergarten children, five and six years of age. I had never seen such large five and six year olds in my life! Parents wanted so much for their children to learn that they would agree to any age in order for the child to be enrolled. Attempting to register the children was an exercise in futility. It was difficult to spell the names, and the parents did not always know or pretended not to know the year their child was born. Consequently, we took as many as we could; in my class there were twenty to twenty-five of the most loving, charming, eager, and engaging children that one could hope for.

Teaching itself was different on Ebeye, obviously. We had a format to follow: the first assignment was to teach the alphabet. I vividly remember how, when I came to the letter C, said "cow," and then asked where milk came from, a little voice peeped up, saying, "Kwajalein." I instantly realized how much deeper I had to dig. We finally established that cows produced milk, and that milk was bottled or canned then shipped to Kwajalein.

Getting to Ebeye was not necessarily easy. We rode the *Tarlang* to Ebeye each morning after our own children were in school, and we returned early afternoon by water taxi before our children came home. Indeed, this was a one of my most rewarding experiences. I loved the children, and they were so eager to learn. Not only did the children learn a great deal, we also learned much from them about their culture. Although I don't know what impact I actually made in that short period of time, there was mutual love and respect.

Since Carl was entering kindergarten and needed me at home, scheduling did not permit me to continue my volunteer work on Ebeye. Needless to say, I did not have the heart to tell them goodbye; I just did not return. When the parents discovered I would no longer be a teacher, they embroidered four hand-made pillowcases and a half slip for me, and brought them to my trailer on Kwajalein. These were thoughtful, beautiful gifts that gave me the measure of these wonderful people. I use the pillow cases to this day.

Chapter 10

WORK and R&R

After Carl went to school, since I did not want to be an idle housewife, I took the offered Civil Service exam. I did this to see if I could get back into the labor market. Eventually, I was hired by the Corps of Engineers, and worked as an administrative assistant under the direction of the greatest boss, Leo T. Baldwin.

In this administrative office, there was a group of very intelligent people who had worked around the world; I had never met people who had worked outside the continental U.S. for fifteen or twenty years or more. These were well-traveled, adaptable people who had great stories to tell. I learned much from these world travelers, most importantly respect for peoples all around the world. Thus, my reentry into the working world was enlightening and satisfying. Other huge benefits were the close proximity of the job to my trailer, and the ability to take time off for travel. These were benefits beyond compare.

Although we were absorbed in the island life, enjoying our new jobs, schools, and other entertainment, we still needed our relaxation period, and that entailed our every-six-month travel to the lovely islands of Hawaii — different and necessary. Notwithstanding the fact that Kwajalein was a wonderful place to be, one needed a respite from all of this. With fall approaching, the calendar indicated it was time to plan our first R&R trip to Hawaii, which meant two things, *rest* and *relaxation* — and purchasing items not available on Kwajalein for yourself and friends. We were excited!

There were hair, eye and dental appointments to keep, and more sightseeing on Oahu. No one left for R&R without a shopping list for Long's Drug Store and the Food Market. Our vacation plans were to visit the Big Island of Hawaii at the historic Volcano House, spend several days on Maui at the Maui Sands Motel, then go on to Poipu Beach Resort on the Garden Island of Kauai.

With appointments made and shopping lists in hand, we left for Honolulu. We flew first to the Big Island for our stay at Volcano House. No matter how many times one sees this, one cannot but marvel at the magnificent scenery; the beauty was unbelievable. Volcano House is noted for its continuous fire in its oversized fireplace. We were told that this fire is never extinguished: even through renovations, embers are saved for the new fire.

Naturally, we visited the birthplace of King Kamehameha and the statue erected in his memory, and we also visited Captain Cook's monument and the City of Refuge. Finally, we went to the beach, which was nothing like those of New Jersey. The Kalapano black sand beach was so very different; in contrast to the white sands of New Jersey, the black sands were an unusual beauty. Just imagine an entire beach of black sand with the blue ocean, and white foam as the water breaks to the shore! My first look at the black sand, I found truly amazing — it was shiny and ebony black, and I felt its powdery softness as I cupped it in my hands and allowed it to flow through my fingers. Obviously, we were all awestruck by this wondrous act of nature.

Because this was a place created by volcanoes, the forests, vegetation, parks, and waterfalls were all unforgettable and truly different. It is difficult to imagine the greatness of the Akaka Falls, a waterfall that is slender and plunges over a deep cliff into a gorge. On the east side is Hilo, a city that exports sugar, coffee, and rice. Since we wanted to visit both coasts, we departed Hilo and headed for the Kona coast, where delicious Kona coffee is grown, but which is also famous for macadamia nuts and fruits such as papaya and bananas. In addition, plantations and cattle ranches are numerous on these islands.

After our tours, we flew to Maui, which easily became my favorite island. The whaling town of Lahaina was like a picture book. It is a quaint seafaring town, and great for whale watching. There was the largest banyan tree on the island, and many valleys, waterfalls, and bays. We stood in the valley and looked up at the mountains, and became involved in a most serene, calming, and spiritual experience. The beauty is indescribable — one could say that the island was beyond beautiful. Because the island is very large, we drove for hours to reach Hana through lush valleys and tropical landscapes, stopping to enjoy beautiful flowers like the bird-of-paradise growing in the wild, fern grottos, and wonderful, flowing waterfalls. What must Eden have been like!

Our first look at the massive banyan tree; Lahaina, Maui, Hawaii

Bernie drove up the narrow nerve-testing road to Haleakala Crater so we could witness the depth of the crater, and it was spectacular: at least a 4000-foot view nearly straight down into the Pacific Ocean. That scene was multiplied in several varied scenes of wonderment in this paradise. Consequently, Maui remains my favorite island. There is almost a spiritual closeness with the beauty and the vastness of that island.

Besides the awesome beauty of Maui, Kauai was also spectacular. One could easily see why it is called "the garden island." There were the most gorgeous, colorful, and sweet-smelling flowers on Earth — the spicy fragrance of the carnation and the perfumed gardenia were the most potent. The flowers in the fields were bright, with yellow plumerias, pikake, white ginger, and purple vandal orchids, just to name a few of these exotic flowers. No other place on Earth could have a display of assorted flowers as beautiful and as sensual as these.

Indeed, we were surrounded by indescribable splendor. We visited Waimea Canyon, called "the Grand Canyon of the Pacific" because the hues were so much like those of the canyons in Arizona — soft orange, ruddy red, tan, and other earth tones. While there, we visited the Fern Grotto, saw sugarcane fields, and stopped and sampled the sweet stalks. This was a relaxing time for us, and we had an excellent look at three of the most popular outer islands.

Shopping, dental appointments, and hair appointments were also necessary, however; thus, our final stop was to Oahu, where Brenda and I went to Queen Street, a less attractive area of Oahu not usually frequented by tourists. It is, however, where the locals live and shop, and was the area in which our hair appointments were made. We had been told of this coveted location by our current beautician at the Regency Hotel, who was leaving the business and wanted to help us in our distress. While we were getting beautiful — beauty meaning that we each had our hair relaxed and set — Bernie and the boys went to Long's Drug Store with the list.

Later, we took Mark to the dentist for his major dental problems.

Mark and I had made several trips into Honolulu for the dentist to determine if an extraction and braces were needed. After this determination, we went shopping for clothes. Clothes shopping for the children brought them the latest in fashion, which may have been in limited supply on Kwajalein: jeans, surfers, bathingsuits, and shirts for the boys; and jeans and a couple of new muumuus for Brenda and myself. As usual, Bernie required very little — a new aloha shirt or two.

This was followed by food shopping. Hard-to-get items on Kwajalein were most important. How many jars of Ragu spaghetti sauce you could carry for yourself and friends became a major problem. Uncle Ben's long-grain rice was a product I purchased, as well as assorted hard cheeses. Not only food was purchased, but also other essentials, such as bridge tallies and cocktail napkins; they were always in short supply. At Long's Drug Store, we purchased everything from toothpaste, Ambersol, aspirin, skincare products, personal items, and various other things. This completed, we were ready to return to Kwajalein. We considered our first R&R trip a huge success.

Chapter 11

PREPARATIONS for TRAVEL

Living on Kwajalein had many advantages; two excellent reasons to reside outside of the United States, aside from the interesting and important work, were tax-exempt status and the ability to accumulate vacation days. From this location, people easily took long, exotic vacations; visiting Australia, New Zealand, or Japan was not unusual. Some people traveled around the world, and in 1967, we decided to join that latter group. Because our tour of duty had been extended, we accumulated many vacation days.

The children were now twelve, eleven, and seven, perfect ages for exposure for travel and enjoying and learning about other cultures — just as they had absorbed so much from the Kwajalein culture. Thus, while on R&R in 1967, we visited a travel agency that specialized in world travel to discuss a possible trip.

Having a family of five proved to be invaluable: we constituted a "tour group," enabling us to take advantage of our family's size. Plans for the trip were both exciting and stressful — so many things to consider, so many countries, so many clothes, so many cultures and deadlines to meet. Our first stop from Kwajalein would be Honolulu, then on to Japan on the 16th of June, 1968; we would then cross the International Dateline, lose a day, and arrive in Tokyo on a Monday night. There were so many plans to make.

We purchased coats from catalogs, since we had given ours away before leaving New Jersey, and we purchased numerous other items necessary for travel. We were warned to take soft toilet tissue and other items that were not available in foreign countries. Since we wanted our luggage to be conspicuous, we purchased apple green so as to distinguish it quickly, a very important aspect when traveling and locating luggage. We read as much as possible, and we each picked out something we just had to see in a particular country. So, on the 16th of June, we began our journey to visit nineteen countries in a little over two months.

Japan

Chapter 12

TOKYO, JAPAN

Tokyo, the exotic city we had read about and experienced in our dreams was finally a reality. Everything went as planned; we survived the long plane ride and arrived in Tokyo at nine o'clock at night. Fortunately, our Japanese travel agent was waiting for us with a sign reading, "Welcome to the Darrell Family." However, the agency was not prepared for us with their small cab; ultimately, we took two taxi cabs to get us to the Maranuchi Hotel in the business district of Tokyo.

That first night, we had dinner in the hotel. It was comical. Bernie ordered a typical Japanese dinner, with fish, tempura, vegetables, and rice. We spent the dinner hour laughing at his valiant efforts to use the chopsticks. Because we were intimidated by the chopsticks, the children and I ate an American dinner, with a promise to try chopsticks the following day. To the children's pleasure, they found that American cartoons had been dubbed into Japanese, and they thoroughly enjoyed their first night in Japan. Plus, the Japanese beds were low, close to the floor, and they found that interesting and created a game of rolling off the bed.

The next day, we began our exciting exploration of this exotic city. What struck me most the following day was the number of cars and the number of people on the streets. It seemed as though we and they were mesmerized by each other. We stared at the crowded scene and at them, and they stared at us; obviously, they were not accustomed to seeing Negro people, and consequently, we immediately became our own private circus.

Now, this was a challenge; we understood nothing, not menus, street signs, billboards, nothing! Similarly, we did not speak the language, and at that time, very few Japanese spoke English. Knowing this was going to be a quest, we carried the hotel's business card to show cab drivers where we would eventually want to return, but sometimes that did not work. For instance, once, a kind Japanese man had to come to the cab and read the card and explain our destination to the cab driver. Thank God for that man! Needless to say, the language barrier was horrendously frustrating for us. Today, however, one of my sons speaks Japanese.

Finally, we went to the American Embassy seeking help from a friend, but it was closed. So much for help. We continued to attract attention because of the children and our color. I remember people being polite, disciplined, and curious about us, but not overly friendly. Undoubtedly, the Japanese were that way toward all foreigners, since they were a relatively closed society — much less so today, with people traveling so very much.

Japanese cab drivers lunching in the "peace and quiet" of a cemetery

We decided to take a tour of the city on our own, and enjoyed the adventure. We strolled the Ginza, and marveled at all the Sony and other electronic products available. We marveled at shops squeezed into tiny spaces side-by-side, reminding us of stores along Broadway in New York City. The city itself was so modern, yet we saw women in pretty kimonos cinched at the waist with obis, some even carrying parasols.

The majority of women were in western dress much like we were dressed. We were to discover, the new and old came together often in Japan. We saw pachinko game parlors and all kinds of pinball machines, and at night the Ginza looked like our Times Square, ablaze with neon lights. The lights added frivolity to the night, and people appeared more relaxed and friendly than they had been during the day.

Before arriving in Tokyo, we had planned several tours with English-speaking tour guides. We began our tour with a visit to the Tokyo Tower, after which we ate at the Hap-po-en restaurant, where Bernie, refusing to admit defeat, tried again to use chopsticks. Eventually he succeeded with tiny morsels, but continued to fail terribly with rice. We gave him an "E" for effort, particularly since we had yet to try.

Our real adventures began the next day, with our bus trip to Nikko. It was an entire day's trip, and we had a wonderful panoramic ride that gave us a sweeping view of the farming areas and rice paddies. I was amazed at the amount of labor that women did, and decided that we Americans were spoiled. For example, these women were bent over in the paddies, their heads covered with wide-brimmed hats, tending the rice fields.

After watching them work, we visited the Sacred Bridge, the fabulous Yomeinom Gate, and the Three Monkey Carvings. The drive included thrilling hairpin curves and so many more things that I can't remember all that we saw, but we returned to Tokyo that night, absolutely thrilled by our exciting day in Japan.

KAMAKURA and HAKONE

The following day, we had another excursion with our English-speaking guides to Kamakura and Hakone. At Kamakura, we visited Daibutsu, the great statue of Buddha, which was far more than we expected: the image was huge and imposing — forty-two feet high — made of bronze, and sat with his hands resting in the position of faith. For seven centuries, this Buddha had drawn visitors to Kamakura, and we now understood why they had been so attracted.

Daibutsu Buddha at Kamakura; his size overwhelmed us.

After visiting the Buddha, we were off to Lake Hakone, where we got our first good view of the majestic, magnificent Mount Fuji. What can I say to describe such magnificence?

We stopped for lunch after our beautiful day, and dined at a restaurant that displayed Japanese graciousness and served excellent tempura. We ate shrimp, carrots, string beans, and sweet potatoes, all fried in their famous tempura batter. Chopsticks were easier to use with the firmer, larger pieces of food; although we used them, we had by no means mastered the art.

Following the delicious lunch, we took the bullet train back to Tokyo. The loading of the train exceeded the cramming of people onto trains in New York. Unbelievably, they had actually hired employees to shove passengers in the doors. That was a real job.

KYOTO

After Kamakura and our exciting visit there, we flew to Kyoto, the first capital of Japan, to see the old Imperial Palace and tour the city. On our first evening, we went to Gion Corner to see demonstrations of traditional Japanese arts: flower arranging, a tea ceremony, and a puppet show. For some reason, the Japanese tour guides thought we wanted to see an American jazz show, and we had to convince them that we wanted to see something of their culture; we were persistent, though, and succeeded.

Another evening, we attended one of the traditional and most revered night performances of the Sumo wrestlers. These giant men dominated the ring with the size and strength of their massive bodies, yet they appeared so agile. Needless to say, we enjoyed the performance and were delighted to have witnessed one of Japan's most cherished sports.

One of our last tours was a peculiar visit to us — a trip to a Tokyo cemetery, where among the dead were lines and lines of taxi cabs. Obviously, we were surprised, but our guide said it was part of a custom; the drivers came to eat lunch and enjoy some peace and quiet. Since this was our last day in Japan, I felt glad about all I had seen, but was sad and frustrated about the magnitude of the language barrier. Unfortunately, we were becoming accustomed to being our own private circus: the Japanese had the longest staring ability, but we found it all quite amusing.

Hong Kong and Thailand

Chapter 13

HONG KONG, CHINA

Finally, we left crowded Japan for the even more crowded Hong Kong. If we thought Japan was exciting and exotic and crowded, then Hong Kong was the epicenter. What an exciting city!! There were people, people, and even more people, but at least one could read the signs, billboards, and menus, which was a major plus. Fortunately, our accommodations were at the Empress Hotel, a magnificent place, and moreover, these Asians were gracious hoteliers. They pampered their guests with every possible amenity — and, needless to say, we enjoyed their pampering immensely.

Hong Kong Floating Market, Village of the Boat People

Unlike Tokyo, Hong Kong lent itself to much more pleasurable tours. Our first day of tours took us to Kowloon and the New Territories, and consisted of a 56-mile scenic drive through industrial Kowloon, its beaches, terraced paddy fields, and plantations. We passed close to the Bamboo Curtain, and somehow, this made me nervous.

Hong Kong, a British protectorate at the time, had a different feeling: it was lighter and happier. The people were less formal than the Japanese, more relaxed, and eager to show their country; plus we felt more comfortable with their use of the English language. In this shopper's paradise, most of the streets were filled with little shops that sold cameras, computers, games, jewelry, and custom-made clothing. Hong Kong was made for shoppers like me. Though the feeling was light and happy, the people seemed in a hurry, so much so that one almost felt like walking in step with the hurrying people. Selling and shopping made everyone happy, plus the staring here was less intense.

Shopping was the main focus in Hong Kong. Salesmen stood in the doorways of fabric shops and beckoned you inside as though they were welcoming you into their homes. Somehow, a chair appeared from somewhere for your comfort, and then with great gestures, they produced bolts of fabric and gallantly unfolded it in front of you for your approval. While you looked and tried to envision a garment made of the fabric before you, a can of Coke or some other drink was offered for refreshment. They do all of this with graciousness and true hospitality. Amazingly, after you have made a selection, you are told that the custom-made garments would be ready for pick up the next day. Bernie, though hesitant at first, had suits and several monogrammed shirts made. I managed to select fabric for a beaded evening gown and a Harris Tweed coat for our return to the States. At the custom shoe shop, Bernie had "dressy" navy shoes made for special occasions, and I ordered a pair of dark green leather shoes and a matching handbag. The quality was excellent, and Bernie wears his shoes to this day.

After all the shopping, we still had sightseeing to do, since this was a wonderful city to explore. Hong Kong is divided into sections, and because of this, we hardly knew where to start. Our sightseeing guide suggested we do the Aberdeen Village first. In this village, the people live on boats:

houseboats, junks, and sampans. Clearly, that was the largest fish market we had ever seen. Initially, we took a ride on a sampan to get a closer look at the community of boat people. Watching people wash their clothes, bodies, and fish for food in these waters was an amazing scene. They cooked food on their boats; I have not yet figured out how they sat down for a meal, since everything was so close, so lacking in space, but they seemed comfortable in their environment.

For our meal in this quaint village, we chose Hong Kong's famous Floating Restaurant in Aberdeen Harbor, known for its extraordinary seafood and view of the fishing village. Bernie, a lover of duck, chose crispy Peking duck, and thought his selection outstanding. The children selected American fare, and I selected a fish that was highly seasoned and delicious. Although I cannot remember its name, the fish was beautifully prepared and presented. We continued to watch the boat people from the restaurant; since the floating restaurant was anchored in the harbor, we had full view of their activities while we dined.

After lunch, we took the Star Ferry to Hong Kong Island. On Hong Kong Island, we rode the tram to Victoria Peak, where there were many beautiful homes and restaurants, as well as an amusement park. There was a magnificent view of the skyscrapers, the harbor, and the famous Happy Valley Racetrack. At night, Aberdeen harbor seemed to be the most beautiful harbor in the world; the port was ablaze with lights, and we breathlessly surveyed the spellbinding sight. It was captivating.

The next day, we picked up our garments and did more shopping in those fascinating shops. Since jade is a favorite Chinese gem, we bought jade for me and pearls for Brenda, to be presented on her sixteenth birthday. Because we had much more traveling to do, we mailed our purchases to our APO address. Having immersed ourselves in as much of the

Chinese culture as we could, and having shopped, toured, dined, and had clothes tailored, we finally said farewell to Hong Kong and boarded our plane to Thailand.

Chapter 14

THAILAND

We arrived in Bangkok, Thailand, in the afternoon via Air India. After we had settled in at the Princess Hotel, we relaxed and read literature about this country. Since we were somewhat exhausted and it was late, we ate dinner in the hotel and prepared ourselves for the full tour the following day. We discussed *baht*, the Thai currency, and wondered if we would be able to use it correctly. Changing currency in each country was always a great challenge.

Bangkok's Floating Market along the Chao Phana River

Similar to Hong Kong, Thailand, too, had a floating market. It was mostly like the Fishing Wharf in Aberdeen, Hong Kong, only the Thai living quarters seemed to be backed on the river for easy access. Again, debris was floating in the water, as vendors sold their wares and bathed in the same

Chao Phana River. They sold fruits, vegetables, flowers, and a variety of other things. Frankly, we found it quite unusual that we could float down the river and look into their thatched-roof living quarters at the same time. The houses on the banks of the river were on stilts, and it was interesting to see them close up.

We visited the site of the Temple of the Dawn, also known as *Wat Arun* or *Dawn Pagoda*; it is one of Thailand's most famous temples. Because it was under renovation, we were not allowed to enter, but our guide happily told us that the United States was helping to pay for the renovation, and they were extremely grateful to our country. The Temple of the Dawn, however, is decorated on the exterior with pieces of porcelain and tiles used on ships arriving from China.

Another interesting tour, very near the Temple of the Dawn, was of the Reclining Buddha, the size of which astonished us. This Buddha was one hundred fifty feet long and fifty feet high. Although gold leaf covers her exterior, under the gold leaf is plastic and brick; her eyes were mother-of-pearl, and she was overwhelming in her position of repose.

Here, too, we attended a nighttime performance of native dance where the costumes were colorful and exquisite. The dancers were beautiful and extremely graceful, and the music and dancers were in perfect harmony. It was a stunning performance, and our eyes were riveted to the stage and performers. Each country has its own dances and costumes, and Thailand's were extraordinarily attractive.

Moreover, because the elephant is valued and revered in Thailand for its strength and usefulness, we made a visit to an outdoor arena to watch trained elephants display their strength and intelligence, moving logs across the water on command. While the children were thrilled with their gentleness, strength, and beauty, they also wanted to experience a ride on an elephant, which they eventually did.

After a wonderful day of sightseeing, the following day, a Sunday, we had to find a Roman Catholic church for mass — this we always do, no matter where we are in the world. The concierge in the hotel directed us to a mission used by the military. The priest was so delighted to see a family, especially with children, that he centered his homily around us. We were one family among all the soldiers. Of course, he asked us where we were from, and admired us for being there.

Before departing Thailand, we purchased many temple rubbings of elephants, horses, and dancers to give as souvenirs; these proved to be a valuable gift, very presentable when framed.

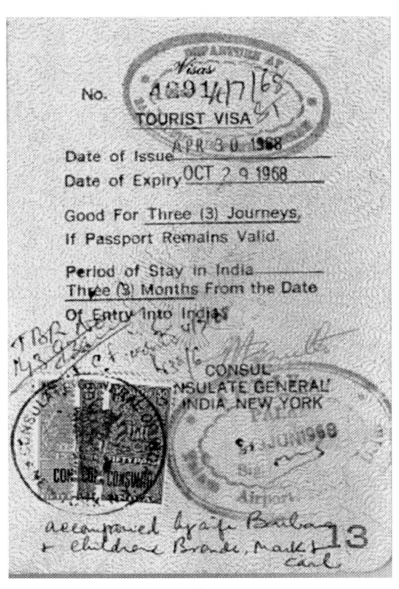

India

67

Chapter 15

NEW DELHI, INDIA

Bangkok was our last stop in Thailand before we left for a long anticipated trip to India, to see in all its glory one of the Seven Wonders of the World: the Taj Mahal.

First, of course, we immediately had to adjust ourselves to the local climate, the temperature soaring to around 105° when we arrived in New Delhi at nine o'clock at night. We soon learned that this was typical Indian weather. Again, we were met by our representative, and were transferred to the Ambassador Hotel. We had a relaxing morning and began touring in the afternoon.

While the elephant was king in Thailand, the water buffalo was revered in India. I will never forget, however, the cows being led around the beautiful, circular, pink Parliament House to eat grass; cows were used in place of lawnmowers — imagine! The avenues in that district were broad and tree-lined, and the Central Secretariat, a prominent temple, a Shopping Center, and the Race Club were in the area.

On one tour, we did some walking; we asked our driver to stop the car to allow us a walk through a neighborhood and absorb the local atmosphere, if that was permitted. We wanted to be closer to the people for just a few moments, and immerse ourselves in their daily lives. Once again, just as we had in Japan, we became our own private circus. People stopped and stared at us; some wanted to touch us, and all were curious about the cameras and recording machines in our use.

We were a strange sight in this country as we strolled among the young and old beggars and the idle people. Some began to crowd us for closer inspection, and at one point, Carl became very upset because he felt smothered. Here we were in the "neighborhood," taking pictures when permitted, recording every word the guide said, and naturally, people were curious. I had to take Carl aside and explain to him that if the scene was reversed, would he not be curious if he saw a woman dressed in a sari walking down Farmdale Road, taking pictures and recording? I think it had been the closeness of the crowd that unsettled him, but he took the rest of the tour in stride.

As usual, I found time to do a little shopping, my great pleasure. Not every person or district in India is poor; very fine silks, some embroidered in gold, were sold in the shops, as well as fine jewelry. I purchased a silk sari embroidered in eighteen carat gold, and a piece of blue silk fabric likewise embroidered. I was advised to never get rid of the sari, and if I did, to make sure that the fabric was melted down and the gold saved. The sari is still in my possession, however, and has hardly been used, though it is still beautiful and often admired.

AGRA, INDIA

Although New Delhi was large and unusual, our greatest excitement was the anticipation of seeing the Taj Mahal. It was a long ride to Agra where the Taj is located, however, and we had a crazy driver, a real hot rod; I termed that trip, "Our Crazy Ride to Agra." He truly thought he was king of the road; about twenty-five years of age, he was turbaned, and felt all-powerful behind the wheel of a vehicle. He drove like a bat out of Hades, and we were scared most of the way. Actually, he hit a dog, and we all screamed; however, the driver stopped only long enough to pick the dog up and throw it along the wayside. He immediately jumped back in the car and never said a word. We were horrified!

As we continued on the road to Agra, the streets and roadways took on a new look, as if the pages of National Geographic had opened up. The landscape was an unbelievable sight — it was teeming with people. There were people everywhere: men, women, children, babies, and young girls carrying babies. In my life, I had never seen so many people on the streets in one locale. People were scantily dressed, men primarily in their *dhoti* (loin cloths), and all were obviously in need. Poor people sat along the road, eating, sleeping, selling wares, nursing babies — young and old begging, just barely existing. I now understand why Mother Theresa was so sorely needed.

As if this were not overwhelming enough, there were also men with snakes around their necks, meandering along with dogs, cats, cows, and sacred water buffalo. It was a scene that, had I not witnessed it, I would not have believed could exist. It was so extremely heart-wrenching; yet we noticed billboards advising birth control and suggesting Planned Parenthood looming above the crowded squalor. They were aware of their overpopulation problem, and the necessity of curbing its growth.

THE TAJ MAHAL

When we arrived at the site of the Taj Mahal, one of the Seven Wonders of the World, what our eyes beheld amid its peace and splendor was worth the horrendous drive to Agra. Never, never, had I seen anything so magnificent! We were spellbound and just awestruck by the beauty.

The Taj Mahal sits in a garden of dark cypress trees with shady lawns and reflecting pools. It is made of a pearly white marble, but its reflection of the sunlight gave it a pink glow. Some call this the "monument of love" because Emperor Shah Jehan built it in memory of his wife, Queen Mumtaz Muhal, who died during childbirth. The monument took twenty-two years to build. It had to have been a labor of the truest love, for we found it difficult to depart the site of such incomparable beauty, but go on we did. We wanted to try to take the road from Agra before night fell. Needless to say, we were unnerved when we entered the vehicle of the hot rod. We returned safely to New Delhi, however — thank God.

Late afternoon sun casts a pink glow over
the magnificent Taj Mahal

The following day, we were to visit the Fort, built in 1563; it, too, was a magnificent palace, with courtyards, audience halls, and private chambers. Seemingly, the Indians used marble to the utmost degree, as marble from ancient lime quarries had been widely available. Many of their buildings were made of white marble and inlaid with semi-precious stones native to the area. Contrasts in India were so extreme — from the people, to the architecture, to the topography, the variety is tremendous.

Another remarkable tour was of the great Mahatma Gandhi's tomb, a visit that we shall forever treasure. The day we visited, it was 110° in the shade. To approach the tomb, we

71

had to remove our shoes and don foot covers so as not to scratch the marble walks. The monument was simple in design, and appropriate to the man; its color was a deep blue, almost black. One could actually feel that he had been a man of peace — the monument seemed to exude peace and serenity, as though describing the soul of the man. Bernie and I both remembered when Gandhi died, and his tomb exemplified for us this man of peace. To see where he was interred seemed to truly place it in history for us.

"It was 110 degrees in the shade when we visited the Memorial."

BOMBAY/MUMBAI

We left New Delhi for a quick flight to Bombay — which, as of the 5th of February, 1996, was renamed *Mumbai*. Arriving at eleven o'clock in the morning and having limited time, we began touring immediately.

Marine Drive was the city's splendid promenade by the sea. It was a beautiful place to stroll in the evening, since it embraced the Bay of Bombay. Part of our tour took us to an area belonging to the Parsi Indians. The female guide explained to us that the Parsi do not bury the dead underground; instead, they hoist the body into the air on poles, and leave it to be consumed by vultures. Presently called "the Tower of Silence," the site is made of rock with a pit in the middle; the area is closed to outsiders. Their belief is that fire, water, and earth are sacred, and a corpse would defile the earth. The guide also stated that vultures devour a body in two days or less. I could not get the image of a body being pulled apart by vultures out of my mind; it still makes me flinch.

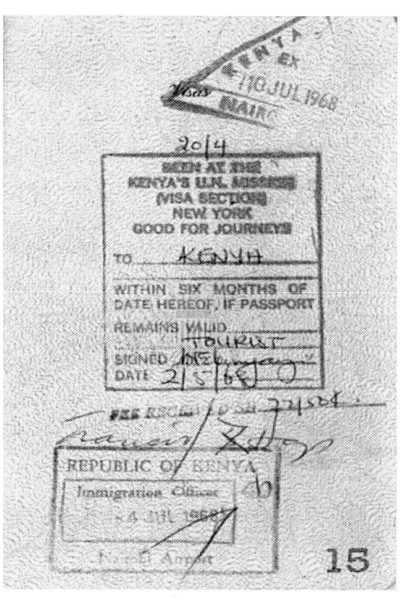

Kenya

Chapter 16

NAIROBI, KENYA

Having exhausted our time in Bombay, we ventured onto another continent and a totally different culture. In Africa, we visited Nairobi, Kenya. We arrived there at three o'clock in the afternoon and were met by our representative, who took us to the fabulous Norfolk Hotel, a five-star hotel that was once the haunt of the gentry. To think — we were staying at the same hotel frequented by Ernest Hemingway. Because there were five of us, we were assigned to one of the cottages, an entire small house for our family. What comfort and convenience, especially for the children!

Despite the ambience and spaciousness, we had all our meals in the splendid, elegant dining room of the Norfolk, a short walk from our cottage. The two bedrooms, the bathroom, and the large living area were hospitable after we had been confined to one or two hotel rooms in our earlier travels. We thoroughly enjoyed the Norfolk Hotel cottage.

When entering the dining room for the first time, we were so impressed by the greeting "Jambo," which means "welcome," and the wide, warm smiles we received from the waiters. At each meal, we felt truly welcome when we were greeted with "Jambo"; the graciousness, the delectable food and its presentation, plus the level of service were extraordinary, and will always be remembered.

President Jomo Kenyatta had been Kenya's president only since 1963, and from my tourist's point of view, he was doing a wonderful job. Nairobi was a beautiful city, clean, modern, and thriving, with a downtown comparable to any other city. The business area had stores filled with current merchandise, and people seemed businesslike and happy.

The roads in the city were well paved, and had colorful flowers in their median strips.

Since Nairobi is a mile-high city, the temperature was always cool, and this coolness was a welcome change from the heat we had endured in India. Moreover, as African-Americans in Africa, we did not attract the attention we had in other countries. Little Carl seemed to be disappointed by the lack of attention. We got a big laugh out of this, and told him he looked more like these folks, so we were not such an oddity.

The atmosphere in Nairobi was warm and friendly, and we felt welcome everywhere. Our first tour was of the Nairobi National Park, which is a 44-square-mile park within the city's boundaries. Needless to say, it had many wild animals, such as elephants, cheetahs, and rhinos, but it was most famous for its lions. The fact that the park was so close to the cosmopolitan city, yet the animals were not confined as in our zoos, was amazing to us. The animals roamed freely as in their own habitats.

SAFARI, MASAI, and KILIMANJARO

A picture-taking safari was on our agenda for the following day; this took us through the countryside, where we saw waterfalls, mountains, and forests. We rode in a van designed for picture taking. Our guide drove us through the bush to view rhinos, elephants, and many other game species. A rhino tried to charge our van, but was unsuccessful; as we sped off, the guide told us that rhinos can't see from a distance, so we had nothing to fear.

We were fortunate enough to see a lion kill; however gory, it was interesting. While the lion was pulling the intestines from a gnu, Bernie snapped pictures as quickly as he could. Clearly, we shall never forget the scene, because we have the most wonderfully explicit pictures. Although we thought the scene gory, we were witnessing actual life in the bush. Where else could we observe this most unusual scene?

The lion kill; only in the bush could this be witnessed!

The lion devours the intestines of a Gnu

After the lion devoured most of the animal, he shared parts with his pride. Though he is really king of the jungle, the lion lacks the speed of a cheetah. We felt our guide was an expert in finding the most interesting sights, and he was so proud of this find to share with us. Similarly, we felt that he, too, was of interest: he had an elongated (stretched) earlobe, which had been split, and surely hung to his shoulder when not folded. However, that day it had been folded several times, and in the hole he had left open sat a small box of matches. I covered Carl's mouth quickly enough to prevent him from yelling out about what he too, had noticed.

After a good night's rest, our driver drove southward the next day, across the Athi Plains to the Amboseli Game Reserve. The game reserve is about 25 miles from the Tanzanian border, and on good days, one should be able to see the famed Mount Kilimanjaro. Our guide informed us that the grasslands here were lower, making it easier to spot elephants and giraffes from a distance. We had a full day of game spotting, frequently seeing herds of gnu, zebras, elephants, and giraffes. I never dreamed it would be so fascinating! On the spot, I developed a new respect and love for wildlife, and a fascination with the giraffe.

Our tour had arranged for us to spend one night in a hotel in Amboseli and the other in a safari tent similar to those often seen in the movies: our guide was at the hotel in the morning, ready to continue our search for animals. Thus, we spent the morning viewing black rhinos, wildebeests, giraffes (now my favorite), elephants, and lightning-fast cheetahs. We viewed a herd of zebra. I cannot explain the thrill of seeing animals in their natural habitats; zoos and wild animal farms cannot duplicate its thrill.

Because it was also Masai country, we visited a Masai village in the hope of meeting these interesting tribesmen. The Masai live in low huts made of brush and plastered with cow dung. Additionally, the huts are set close together, as it is their custom to live close to each other with their herds in view. Since the number of animals they possessed was a symbol of their status, we were able to discern who was wealthiest in the area.

We saw the Masai women in their native dress: a bib of colorful beads in red, orange, blue, green, and white, beads that the women had strung; some of the women had enlarged earlobes, with holes in the center that contained some form of ornament. In addition, many of the men had spears and shields made of skin, but their garments covered the loin and appeared to be draped over one shoulder. All were covered in some fashion, except the children, who had their torsos exposed.

Carl, a Masai tribesman, and Mark in Masai country,
July, 1968

We loved the children with their smiling faces; they motioned for us to take their pictures, and at once broke out into a spontaneous dance for us, which was mostly jumping up and down and laughing, and then they suddenly stopped and extended their hands for money. Although the red dirt of the earth was embedded in their hair and crusted on their faces, they danced; as they danced, they swatted the circling flies that swarmed around their faces.

As cute as the children were, they were cunning, and did trick us. We gave them money for the dances and told them we wanted to buy some elephant hair bracelets, since elephant hair bracelets were supposed to be good luck. They quickly ran off and returned with the bracelets. At that point, we did not know how to distinguish a genuine elephant hair bracelet from a fake. Brenda and I were happy with our new bracelets, not realizing that they were not elephant hair. Later, at an authentic craft shop, we learned that the bracelets that had delighted us were plastic. Real elephant hair bracelets are softer, more flexible, and carry an odor, especially when wet; there was a huge difference.

Finally pleased, we laughed at the cunningness of the Masai children. At this authentic craft shop, we also purchased a zebra skin, two leopard skins, a small ivory bust of a Masai tribesman, and coasters beaded by Masai women. Fortunately for us, those items could still be taken out of the country at that time.

Although the people were of great interest to us, our most amazing experience were the accommodations in the safari tent. The tents were large, luxurious, and fully equipped, including a manservant. At night, after we retired, the manservant covered our beds with netting reminiscent of the movies. It was truly an unusual experience. To have a formal breakfast — similar to and as good as any served in a five-star hotel — outside in a tent in Nairobi, is truly a rare event. Listening to the various loud and whinny animal sounds of the jungle as we dined was so unusual, a never-to-be-forgotten experience.

We were also attracted by the monkeys screeching overhead, swooping down from the trees, grabbing our sugar cubes from our tables, then jumping back into the trees, swinging happily from limb to limb. Each time the cubes of sugar were replaced, the monkeys would swoop down, quickly grab the cubes, and jump off into the trees again, eating our sugar and laughing. Enjoying these scenes with us was a family of five from Great Britain, who were tented next to us. Our families were happy to meet each other, and thoroughly enjoyed the morning's events as we attempted to enjoy the most delicious breakfast.

We game-watched near the campsite; toward the end of the day, there was a great shout — "Kilimanjaro, Kilimanjaro!" Lo, when the sun finally emerged from the clouds, there stood Mount Kilimanjaro majestically in the background. Indeed, the clouds lifted, and there she was, in all her majesty! What is it that makes a mountain so awesome, so breathtaking? Is it because it is such a wonder of nature, or because it makes one think of the Creator? Each time I see a majestic mountain reveal itself, when clouds are lifted, I am filled with awe.

We thought we were in the movies; the scene could not have been more beautiful — perhaps for us and the British family, it was even more spectacular than any movie we had seen. Nairobi had more than met our expectations. This was another experience never to be forgotten. How fortunate we were, and how especially fortunate and blessed were Brenda, Mark, and Carl.

It was evening when she appeared, and what an awesome
sight — Mount Kilimanjaro, Tanzania

As we were leaving the reserve in our sightseeing van, the
guide told us he had a special sight to show us, even though
we were still amazed from seeing the kill and the mountain.
He swerved the vehicle around; on the road stood a pair of
identical gerenuks, looking straight down the road. Bernie
snapped a picture. Then suddenly, as if on command, the two
gerenuks turned and faced us. Bernie snapped a second
picture. He is still thrilled by that unrehearsed sequence, and
it shows off well in a slide show. Bernie had captured those
beautiful animals to cherish forever.

We left Amboseli with happy and sad hearts — happy for all
that we had experienced, and sad to leave all the wonders of
nature. We were taken back to Nairobi for the night in
preparation for our trip to Uganda.

Two Gerenuks looking down the field

Two Gerenuks looking at the camera — can you spot them?

At the airport in Nairobi, I saw no large planes; we stood around the area waiting for directions or information on our flight. When I saw our apple-green luggage being taken toward a prop plane, I thought, "That can't be our plane." I requested that Bernie go see what was happening.

He came back and stated that it was our plane, knowing full well how afraid I was of planes without four engines. They loaded our apple-green luggage on that sixteen-seat plane, and all the Darrells followed. I prayed all the way across wide Lake Victoria. My negative thoughts were, "If this plane goes down over all this water, our families would never hear of us again." So much water and such a little plane. Even without turbulence, it was not a relaxing flight, and I was overjoyed when we touched down safely in Uganda.

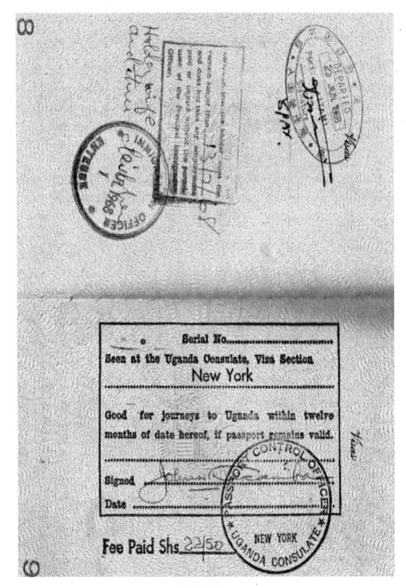

Serial No.....................

Seen at the Uganda Consulate, Visa Section

New York

Good for journeys to Uganda within twelve months of date hereof, if passport remains valid.

Signed ....

Date ....

Fee Paid Shs. 22/50

PASSPORT CONTROL OFFICER
NEW YORK
UGANDA CONSULATE

Uganda

Chapter 17

UGANDA

Our first real disappointment came in Uganda. Bernie had hoped to sail on the famous Lake Victoria, but upon arrival found that the lake was polluted, and was no longer used for recreational purposes. He was crushed. For that reason, we decided to do a few land tours.

We were taken to see many of the lush coffee fields around Lake Victoria and the very green tea plantations of Kampala. Tea and coffee are huge exports from Uganda, since its soil is rich and fertile for such crops. Many Ugandans live and work on family farms, raising sweet potatoes, beans, peas, and maize; they have always owned their land to cultivate, plant, and farm. I can't remember seeing much else; after Bernie's huge disappointment over not sailing, some of the thrill escaped us. Actually, we had gone to Uganda primarily for Bernie to sail on the lake.

However, I do remember having an encounter with our taxi cab driver in Uganda, who, in a condemning voice, accused us of accepting intolerance from white America. I told him, "My country afforded me the opportunity to visit yours." He immediately got the message, and said no more.

Our stay in Entebbe, Uganda, was brief, but it did not go unnoticed that the young waitresses in the hotel would slip out with their hair in natural, kinky curls, and return in about an hour with pressed, straight hair. After watching this happen several times during the day, I spoke with some of the young women about the disappearing act, and was told they were indeed getting their hair pressed, something they learned from Americans. One woman had gone to the States to learn the process, and had set up a little shop nearby. We all had a good laugh; from what I saw, she had a good business going. To attempt to enhance one's beauty is indeed worldwide. Oddly enough, years later, many African-American women began adopting the African style of extremely short or nearly bald haircuts, which are far easier to maintain. Truly, women are vain worldwide.

United Arab Republic

Chapter 18

CAIRO, EGYPT

By the time we departed Entebbe for Cairo, our children were perfect little travelers. When flights did not have assigned seats, they scampered aboard and found seats that they were instructed by us to be the safest. On United Arab Airlines, our transport to Cairo, the children found seats — Mark and Carl together, Mommy and Daddy together, and Brenda with a seat partner.

The plane was packed, and a couple of people were standing. Suddenly, Brenda came back to us to say, "Look what they've done to the boys." Between the two boys sat a man who weighed at least three hundred pounds. We could hardly see little Carl. Bernie got up and told the flight attendant that he had paid for five seats and that is what he wanted; as an argument ensued, streaks of lightning flashed in the windows, and reverberating, rumbling, and crashing noises could be heard surrounding this greatly overbooked flight.

In the first row on the right sat a large woman with a birdcage on her lap; the birds were chirping and jumping around the cage, apparently frightened. The birdcage's holder was also squeezed between two other passengers. The co-pilot asked Mark if he wanted to come up to the cockpit, but Mark refused. Bernie was still standing, arguing in a rather loud controlled voice for the five seats; as thunder boomed and lightning flashed, all I could think was that if the plane was struck by lightning, we would go down with those damn birds flapping over our heads. I developed a new appreciation for American flights, which demanded that hand-carried luggage fit under the seat. The problem was resolved by the fat man going into the cockpit. Needless to say, we were all happy when the episode was over.

We arrived in Cairo in the early hours of the morning. As we deplaned, I remember seeing sun, sand, and more sand — our introduction to the Sahara Desert! We were met and taken to our hotel to have a morning of leisure and begin tours in the afternoon. We decided, however, to take a late morning stroll.

The heat there was unbelievably intense. Bernie donned some blue plaid Bermuda shorts; of course, we didn't think about the fact that the Egyptian men were all wearing caftans — at least, that is what we called them. Now, not only were we our own private circus, but people were laughing at us. For the longest, we could not figure what was so funny. Finally, I saw a couple of men pointing at Bernie and laughing hysterically. I then realized that what was normal wear in most places was outlandish here. We teased Bernie unmercifully about those plaid Bermuda shorts for years.

In the afternoon, properly attired, we visited the Citadel, mosques, bazaars, and monuments. Our guides told us there were over 600 Islamic monuments scattered throughout the metropolis of Cairo. I would not pretend to remember any of the names, but what I do remember is the 12th century alabaster Mohammed Ali mosque, with its dome and slender minaret. Again, we were impressed with the care and love that is given to old edifices in Africa and the Far East.

The bazaars in Cairo caught my fancy, since they had piles of oriental wares. Craftsmen were working brass, ivory, amber, silver, and gold. There were wonderful bargains, and I had learned to dicker by that time and was good at it. I don't remember buying very much, since I had finally learned to buy my charms at reputable gold shops.

One of our adventures in Cairo was a boat ride down the Nile. Again, there was nothing beautiful or tranquilizing about this water. The natives onboard ate, breastfed babies, read, conversed loudly and demonstratively, slept, and gawked at us on the short boat ride. I wondered what Cleopatra would think about the Nile were she living then.

In Cairo, we would visit another of the Seven Wonders of the World: the Pyramids of Giza. When we reached that site of antiquity, we stood there in awe and amazement of what man had been able to do. To finally see those ancient tombs in reality after looking at pictures for years was simply thrilling. We visited and toured them during the day.

Cheops was the only pyramid that could be entered, or climbed on the outside. Cheops was built in the 2600s BC, and is about 450 feet tall. Thousands of slaves worked twenty years to complete its tombs, built to hold the remains of kings. Some of the boulders weighed about 2½ tons each; the second and third pyramids, Chephren and Menkaure, surround the great pyramid, but they are smaller in size.

In his most sincere voice, our guide told us how happy the slaves had been to measure, cut, and deliver these boulders and stones to the site. I smiled and said to myself, "Never in a million years would I believe that!" I made a mental note to take a few tours when we returned home to hear what kind of untruths we tell tourists.

The Darrell family at the Cheops Pyramid

Astride camels, we rode around each pyramid. I did not enjoy the camel ride at all, especially the dismount. Although we had been forewarned, the natives begging in the area were absolutely nerve-wracking. I almost screamed out of fright when so many hands reached for us; however, I was also humbled by the poor, suffering people, who were obviously in dire need. In the Temple Valley near the Pyramids stood the Sphinx: half man, half lion, dominating the area. It is said to be the largest sculpture ever carved by man, and still seems to be a mystery to mankind.

The Sphinx; the "Sound and Light Show"
here was outstanding.

While we were there, we also saw the never-to-be forgotten "Sound and Light Show" of the pyramids at night. We were seated a distance in front of the pyramids, part of an assembly, and out of the darkness of night came a deep, resonant, captivating voice that told of the pyramids and their history. As the voice filled the air, lights are beamed onto the structures, highlighting each as it was described. I heard my daughter say, "Oh, my God," as she put her hands up to her face. The show was magnificent beyond description. Of all the sound and light shows we had seen before and have seen since, that one remains the greatest ever.

While we greatly anticipated visiting the museums — particularly the Cairo Museum, where the King Tut exhibit was housed — we discovered that we had limited and restricted museum visitation due to the 1967 war between Israel and the Arab world. Certain museum areas were off limits; windows were taped, and sandbags were in evidence. However, we were able to see the oldest mummy and learn of the process by which she had been embalmed. Most of their treasures had been secured. Also, because of that war, our agents were unable to book flights to Jerusalem from Egypt. We did not get to Gethsemane, the Mount of Olives, or other Christian shrines as we had planned; this was a huge disappointment, but we went to Beirut, Lebanon, instead.

Lebanon

Chapter 19

BEIRUT, LEBANON

We arrived in Beirut at ten o'clock in the morning. The trip turned out to be a pleasant surprise and one of great interest. Twenty-five miles north of Beirut was the town of Byblos, where examples of every age from the Neolithic to the modern eras can be found. Imagine walking through 10,000 years of history in a single hour! We were told that 10,000 years of continuous life is said to be recorded there.

I remember the flat bread we ate in a Lebanese restaurant, and I believe it is what we now call pita bread; moreover, there were cedar trees in Lebanon, groves and groves of them. I bought a gold charm of a cedar tree for my bracelet; for every gold charm I bought, we purchased one in silver for Brenda. Bernie was collecting currency from each country, and the boys collected pennants from cities and countries for the walls of their bedroom.

In addition to the fact that we were fascinated by each country, since each held its own specific attraction, the memory, beauty, culture, and history of the people that we had seen thus far will remain with us forever. However, the poverty of the people, particularly those in East Africa, India, and Egypt will also remain. We were overwhelmed by the masses of poor. Our visits gave us a different perspective, and we gained a new respect for people who live under substandard conditions, regardless of their country. The struggle to survive under great odds is relentless in those countries. Needless to say, we as a people are totally unaware of these conditions.

Our children saw the differences in their own lifestyle versus those they had observed. Nothing replaces having a story right in front of them to make a lasting impression on the young and old alike. The lower classes, no matter where they live in the world, have a heck of a time trying to pull themselves up by those ever talked about "boot straps." The impact on our family of begging as a way of life was difficult for us to comprehend, especially in 1968. We will never forget the Masai children dancing for money, or the Indian and Egyptian children begging pathetically. You must have a boot.

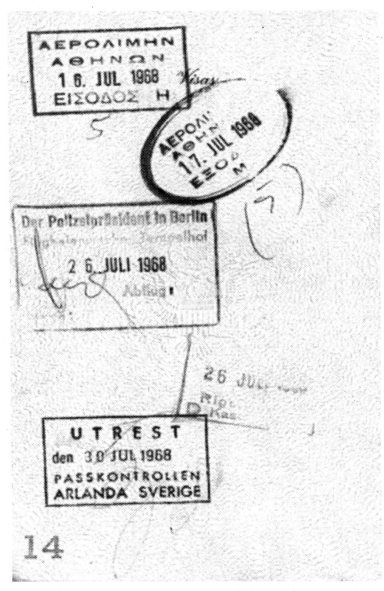

Greece, Germany, and Sweden

97

Chapter 20

ATHENS, GREECE

After intriguing Beirut, we arrived in Athens, Greece, where we stayed in the Acropole Palace Hotel, a lovely place. Like most tourists, we were eager to see the major attractions of Athens — the Acropolis, the Parthenon, and the large theater where great Greek plays had been performed under the night sky thousands of years before.

We stood on the Acropolis, the highest point in Athens, mesmerized by its antiquity, and tried to visualize this site as it had been before Christ; we pictured the Parthenon and the Agora, the marketplace, in their ancient splendor and activity. The Acropolis had first been a fortress in which the people of Greece took refuge; it then became a sacred site when temples to the gods were erected.

The Parthenon, the most famous temple on the site, was erected to honor Athena, the goddess of wisdom and learning. Although the foundation of the Parthenon was made of limestone, its exquisite, graceful columns were carved out of marble. It was there that the statue of Athena was housed. The Parthenon is still considered one of the most beautiful buildings in the world; although it is beautiful in its classic structure, in my opinion, the Taj Mahal is the most beautiful building I have seen in my travels.

The ancient Greek theater was outdoors, and had rows and rows of tiered stone seats that formed a semi-circle around the elevated stage. We walked down a few steps and then sat to get a feel for the hugeness of the theater and a view of the stage. The theaters were so large that most of the audience could not see the actors' faces; therefore, we were told, the actors wore large masks to identify themselves. Many of the ancient Greek theaters have been restored and are used for performances of classical Greek dramas today. We attended a "Sound and Light Show" at the Acropolis, and as impressive as it was, it paled in comparison with the "Sound and Light Show" of the Pyramids.

Our stay in Greece was brief, but Bernie and I managed to have a late-night romantic dinner on the roof of the hotel. Always eager to try new foods, Bernie ordered the recommended eggplant stuffed with ground lamb. Many items were wrapped in grape leaves. The food was delicious, the Greek wine superb, and the lights of the city were spectacular.

Despite all these beauties, incidents do happen. One afternoon, to relax, I removed my girdle and placed it on the night table. After a while, as usual, we decided to do some sightseeing on our own; we left the room and, as in other countries, again we immediately became an oddity. Hours later, when we returned to the hotel, my girdle was gone! I called housekeeping and the front desk, and either they spoke no English or pretended not to. I probably made some woman very happy, since she had a new, slightly-worn girdle. Our stay in Athens was brief, wonderful, yet filled with interest.

Chapter 21

ROME, ITALY

We had great anticipation for the Eternal City of Rome — so many wonderful places and things to see, wonderful old architecture, art galleries, and museums. My heart nearly exploded with excitement as we raced through Customs with passports in hand, so eager to retrieve our luggage and be met by our representative and taken to the Hotel Alexandra.

To our pleasure, Hotel Alexandra was near the Via Veneto, and we were soon strolling the broad, beautiful avenue. It was evening, and the many sidewalk cafés were filled with diners; to our astonishment, we saw that the Italians ate pizza with a fork! Moreover, their pizza was thicker and a more complete meal than ours. We had no trouble eating the foods of Italy; although sometimes prepared differently, we always recognized spaghetti, ravioli, and other Americanized Italian foods.

Aside from gold charms, here I was in pursuit of an Italian knit suit, all important at the time. The entire family joined in this quest, first to locate the boutique, then to make a lovely selection for me. We were successful, and then the serious sightseeing began.

We saw many, many wonderful sights in Rome; the most impressive was St. Peter's Square, and the Basilica within the boundaries of Vatican City. The Vatican is governed by the Pope, and is the smallest independent state in the world. The Sistine Chapel and the frescos painted by Michelangelo were wonders to behold. Our necks ached from looking up and stretching to see all that the ceilings held. It was hard to believe that one man created these paintings, and we again admired the genius and artistry of Michelangelo.

Below the Vatican, in the tombs, stands the Pieta, a statue so beautiful in its simplicity that one stands transfixed, captivated by the message it conveys. The Pieta evokes reverence and silence when one gazes upon this work of art.

Other memorable displays beneath the Vatican were the robes and crowns worn by previous Popes; each Pope's robe was displayed with his name and duration of service. Although styled differently, the robes were all made of elaborate fabric, many woven with threads of gold, yet the folds of the robes fell softly. It was obvious that much care had been given to those robes to ensure that future generations would enjoy them.

The crowns displayed were likewise shimmering with gold and many-colored gems; they were unparalled beauties. I, for one, really appreciated all the history and beauty and artwork before me at the Vatican — works of art by Botticelli, da Vinci, and others. Nothing could rival the magnitude of the splendor at the Vatican Museum, and no one can say enough about the Sistine Chapel.

The following morning, we took a bus tour to the Colosseum, but with all the other tourists, we found it to be far too crowded. Indeed, we were so spoiled. We tried to listen to all the guide had to say as we plotted our return to the Colosseum. That afternoon, we took a taxi and returned to the arena; we were the only ones there, since the Romans were all resting after lunch. We envisioned chariot races and gladiators, and we could almost hear the crowd's roar. I imagined that I heard, "Friends, Romans, countrymen, lend me your ears. I have come to praise Caesar, not to bury him!" We really used our imaginations that afternoon. We had so much fun, and enjoyed our own private tour.

Alone in the Colosseum at noon, we had so much fun!

Several other places were parts of our tour. One of our memorable excursions was to Tivoli — a scenic country ride where we visited Hadrian's Villa, the ruins of the home of Emperor Hadrian. The villa was built around 130 A.D.; it was quite unusual, and among the ruins there was a reflecting pond surrounded by Roman statues.

Another very interesting place was the Olympic Village. In 1960, the summer Olympics were held in Rome, and our tour included a visit to that Olympic Village site. That tour was of special interest to Bernie, who is an ardent track-and-field fan.

Obviously, we had to visit the Trevi Fountain, and, as most tourists do, we threw coins in the fountain while each of us made a wish, one of which was to return to Italy one day.

Visiting the Trevi Fountain in Rome, we tossed coins and made wishes to return someday.

VENICE, ITALY

After Rome we were scheduled to go to Venice, but due to a minor incident with our driver and our luggage, we missed our flight to Venice. In order to transport five passengers and the luggage, the driver strapped some of our luggage onto the roof of his taxi. To our dismay and the driver's disgust, as we were speeding along, one of suitcases fell onto the road, and we had to stop to retrieve our possessions. Spread across the road were the boys' clothing items. Naturally, this delayed our trip to Venice.

To make up for the error, we were flown to Milan with the promise of a car and driver. However, when we arrived in Milan, we were told to take a train. When we refused, a car and driver were provided. The driver was Scottish, spoke perfect English, and was quite personable. Our arrival in Venice had been delayed, but it was a most enjoyable trip despite the mistake.

In fact, we were driven southeast through the Plains of Lombardy, and saw the luscious green landscape and pristine lakes on a more than four-hour ride. It was night when we arrived in Venice, and we took a gondola boat ride down the Grand Canal to the beautiful and elegant old hotel situated on the canal. The employees of the hotel were very welcoming and helpful; thus, it did not take us long to get out onto St. Mark's Square, where a festival was in full progress. Who needed rest?

So much life and fun!! The gondoliers took passengers up and down the canal in their lighted boats, where much singing, dancing, and merry-making abounded, topped off by many displays of unusual and beautiful fireworks. Music and joy filled the air, and we were immediately infected with the festiveness and the spirit of the evening. It was a wonderful way to end a day that had begun with so much frustration.

We had a marvelous time in Venice. The artwork in the pink-and-white marble Doge's Palace occupied us for hours the following day. When we walked around St. Mark's Square, we were intrigued by the glass manufacturers and enjoyed window shopping where the shops were filled with luxurious Italian leather accessories, Italian knits, and artifacts.

We were fascinated by the canals and the gondolas, and from the Square we saw the Bridge of Sighs, the Cathedral, and other points of interest. It was nice to stroll along leisurely, see some of the sights, and observe the people, then stop for a few moments for ice cream gelato. The Italians were so happy and seemed to enjoy life to its fullest, and their exuberance had an impact on us. The atmosphere was as if they had not a care in the world. What a welcome — it was electric!!

Chapter 22

VIENNA, AUSTRIA

Another day, another country. We left Italy and went to beautiful, old Austria, where Vienna was our first stop. Vienna is the city of music, the home of Wolfgang Amadeus Mozart, Johann Strauss, and many other musicians and composers. It was mid-July when we arrived in the lilting, musical city, and we loved Vienna at first sight — who would not?

There we were, in the land where the eight-year-old genius, Mozart, composed symphonies and concerti; in his lifetime, his repertoire contained many operas, sonatas, and works of church music. Johann Strauss, known as "the Waltz King," was famous for his waltzes; "The Blue Danube," one of his most famous, was one I remembered playing on the piano as a child. He, too, came from a musical family. Although his reputation as a conductor was not as renowned, he did write many operettas, polkas, and marches.

Aside from the music, we were most impressed by the architecture of the old buildings; the bakeries and candy shops in the city were also especially tantalizing. We pressed our faces against the sweet shop windows to see what was most appealing to each of us. Never had I seen so many beautifully decorated cakes and candies in shop window after shop window; they simply made me drool. Finally, we decided which shop we should enter, made our selections, and eagerly began to devour the delicacies.

This completed, we headed in the direction of the big Ferris Wheel, which seemed to be visible from everywhere. We made our way onto the big wheel with the help of a kind Viennese woman. Did I ever regret that ride! It was so high and the cars swung out! I vowed never to ride a Ferris wheel again. The children, however, were thrilled; they thought it was the greatest fun ever. The wheel was in a lovely park, and the waltzes of Strauss could be heard floating through the air as the band played its medley. It was an afternoon filled with pleasure.

The woman who helped guide us to the wheel was extremely pleasant, and wanted so much to converse with us. We could speak no foreign languages, and in frustration, Brenda said, "Can't you say anything?" We couldn't, and could not talk with this woman who obviously wanted to know more about us; nor could we talk with any of the many people we met in our travels who wanted to converse. It became embarrassing. I remember thinking, "We Americans must learn foreign languages; most countries of Europe speak French or Italian, but we are limited to English. How arrogant!!" So many people wanted to talk with us, and our high school French and Spanish did not suffice. I think this is the reason two of our children speak foreign languages today.

We decided to immerse ourselves in as much of the music and lives of the composers as we could. Therefore, we visited Mozart's Figaro House, the Schubert Museum, and Beethoven and Schubert's original tombstones. We saw the monuments to Johann Strauss, Brahms, and Mozart. We visited the State Opera House, and were given a demonstration of the acoustics. As in the States, operas are not performed during the summer; to the dismay of our children, neither are there shows of the Lipizzaner horses. A real pleasure for Bernie was his ability to see the original music score of *The Magic Flute*, his favorite opera.

Although the music and the composers were of utmost importance to us, we also took a boat ride to the Vienna Woods, where the woods were lush, green, bountiful, and evoked great Viennese pride. Since Vienna is known for its numerous castles, we saw castles, as well as the spa Baden, which were the healing waters of the ancient Romans. This time, we rushed through Europe as we'd planned; we hoped that we might be able to return there someday. Nevertheless, we enjoyed every city we visited, and Vienna was one of the best.

Chapter 23

BERLIN, GERMANY

After beautiful Vienna, Berlin, Germany, was just as anticipated by us. When we arrived on July 25th, it was gray and unsettling. Immediately, we went on a half-day tour of East and West Berlin. I must admit that I was nervous as we sat on the tour bus in front of Checkpoint Charlie. This was, after all, 1968.

We were instructed not to take pictures, but of course, one American had to snap a picture, which caused the guards to detain us longer than necessary at the checkpoint. Seeing the Wall — all of life split in two by a gray concrete barrier, dividing homes, gardens, and schools — is something I shall never forget.

The Communists erected the wall down the middle of Berlin, dividing the city into two and creating East and West Berlin. We can imagine the depressing effect it must have had on the people, for it was a most gloomy and melancholy sight. I was not comfortable seeing so many Soviet soldiers. At one of our stops, two soldiers picked Carl up, and wanted us to take pictures of them with Carl. They also wanted us to be photographed with them. I was almost paranoid. Bernie worked on radars and missiles, and we were in the midst of a Cold War — I wanted nothing to do with any Soviets, not even as tourists.

THE AMERICAN SECTOR
ВЫ ВЫЕЗЖАЕТЕ ИЗ
АМЕРИКАНСКОГО СЕКТОРА
VOUS SORTEZ
DU SECTEUR AMÉRICAIN
SIE VERLASSEN DEN AMERIKANISCHEN SEKTOR

Bernie at the Berlin Wall

Was I glad to leave that area! Our tour included the
Brandenburg Gate, the Soviet War Memorial, and the Kaiser
Wilhelm Church, a memorial in which a portion remains in
its bombed-out condition. This town really showed how
devastating war could be.

The Kaiser Wilhelm Church, the original and the new;
Berlin, Germany

The Germans were very proud of their new Autobahn highway, which was, to be sure, truly amazing. No one can see Germany without visiting one of its famous beer gardens, which we did and had loads of fun. In this vast hall, there were many jovial, happy, merry people enjoying the evening's festivities. Each of us stood on the wooden benches, as is customary, our arms entwined, swaying and singing with the people, some tourists and many natives. Everyone was having a marvelous time; even the children could enjoy all but the beer.

Although sauerkraut and knockwurst are German, we found out that their sauerkraut and knockwurst are not like ours — ours are better. That was a fun night, and it took some of the edge off of our distressing hours at Checkpoint Charlie. Although it was good to see Germans having a lighthearted evening, I was glad to leave Germany.

Chapter 24

COPENHAGEN, DENMARK

Just as Germany had appeared dark and rather foreboding, Copenhagen, Denmark, appeared to be like a fairytale land, light and magical. We arrived in Copenhagen in our customary manner; however, this was the first time we were disappointed in our accommodations. Although we had two rooms, one was at one end of the hall and the other was at the opposite end. Can you imagine? The bathroom was in yet another location, so we had some adjusting to do! Still our stay wasn't long enough for us to make a fuss, and arriving in Copenhagen was such a weight lifted after being in Germany, to say the least, that we decided not to complain and enjoy the city.

By boat and coach, we traveled through ancient and modern Copenhagen. Magical Tivoli Gardens had to be the most unique amusement park in the world! We had visited Disneyland, and thought it was the epitome in amusement parks, but Tivoli was charming, enchanting, and truly magical. We were able to spend two half-days there, including an evening when the park was illuminated. The beauty cannot be described — the park was dazzling! Not only were the amusements lit, but the gardens, the lake, and the entire park were aglow, and seemed to cast a spell over us all. Also, in that amazing park was a pantomime theater and a concert hall. We loved everything as much as the children did, and Tivoli had to have the best ice cream in the world. The lands of Hans Christian Anderson and the Little Mermaid did not disappoint us at all. The whole city made our hearts glad! It was indeed like a storybook land.

Tivoli Gardens at night — magical day and night
Copenhagen, Denmark

The Little Mermaid represented a storybook realm to us;
we also loved the land of Hans Christian Anderson

Chapter 25

STOCKHOLM, SWEDEN

From Copenhagen, Denmark, it was a quick flight to Stockholm, Sweden. Because Sweden is so far north, it has eighteen hours of sunlight per day in the summer; at ten o'clock at night it looks like three o'clock in the afternoon. Here, too, we were able to cram a lot into our short stay.

After our poor accommodations in Denmark, we had lodging at the Palace Hotel in Stockholm and we were pleased by these accommodations: two adjoining bedrooms and two baths.

After a very short while at leisure, we went on a tour of the Swedish Capitol, the Swedish Pantheon, and the famous City Hall, erected in 1923, with eight million bricks and nineteen million gilded mosaic tiles. Annual Nobel Prize award dinners are held in City Hall, and an elevator took us to the top of the building for a panoramic view of the surrounding areas.

It was pure excitement to enter the beautiful, elegant Concert Hall, where His Majesty the King of Sweden presents the Nobel Peace Prize. My heart was aflutter as I envisioned Dr. Martin Luther King, Jr., being bestowed this honor in 1964. How proud he must have been for himself, his family, his race, and the movement he believed in with all his heart. Being in that hall allowed me to relive that momentous event with a large degree of pride. How sad that his life had come to an abrupt end a few months prior to our visit.

Another great experience that we had anticipated was the smorgasbord. We did not know that smorgasbords were not served during the summer, but we did find one restaurant that was willing to give us the experience. Understandably, we enjoyed the dinner, which consisted of fish dishes, meatballs, cold cuts, breads, assorted cheeses, relishes, and salads. The dishes were served like a buffet; usually, small portions were taken, and the food was tasty and filling. Clearly, we appreciated the restaurant's effort to allow us the experience of a true Swedish smorgasbord. The children especially had fun trying the various dishes. The smorgasbord was another part of the unique culture of Sweden that we experienced and enjoyed.

If the City Hall had been thrilling, the Riddarholm Church, which has been the burial place of Swedish kings for more than 400 years, was even more fascinating. The church was a beautiful medieval structure with a lattice spire that pointed to the sky. Sadly, it was our final stop in Sweden, but we could have remained there for several more days.

England and France

Chapter 26

LONDON, ENGLAND

Finally, to London, England — no language barrier there. It was July 30th, and we were in London, England!! We arrived at twelve-forty five in the afternoon and were transported to the Clifton Ford Hotel. All of us were excited, but I was particularly happy to have the ability to read street signs and the names of the wonderful buildings without referring to a dictionary — an unbelievable pleasure.

Our first tour the following day was to Buckingham Palace, of course, to watch the changing of the guard. The guards march from St. James Palace to Buckingham Palace at 11:30, where the guard changes in front of the palace; we waited for this experience. Buckingham Palace is the residence of the royal family, and therefore, it attracts a large number of tourists as well as locals. The palace, a huge edifice surrounded by high golden gates, contains 600 rooms. Though we did not visit inside, it does, on certain afternoons, allow visitors into the public rooms.

From the palace, we went to Piccadilly Circus, where all the pigeons seemed to have gathered. However, when we reached Trafalgar Square there were even more pigeons, but it was also alive with people and traffic. In the midst of it all was the enormous statue of Admiral Horatio Nelson.

The National Gallery joins the square and houses British masterpieces. Although we were close to it, we had no time to visit the gallery: we had to see the British Prime Minister's residence at Number 10 Downing Street. On the top floor is the residence; and the cabinet offices of the government are on the ground floor. Of course, our visit consisted of standing in front of the building and staring with the other tourists. What else could we do?

The Prime Minister's residence and government offices, Number 10 Downing Street, London

Out of all of this, the pinnacle for me was Westminster Abbey, the building with the most intrigue. It is a beautiful Gothic architecture, where coronations and royal weddings are performed and royals are laid to rest; most impressive to me was the Poets' Corner, where tombs, monuments, and memorials to Tennyson, Shakespeare, Chaucer, and Dickens are in evidence. The remembrances were many; however, Chaucer was the first writer to be buried in the Abbey. I felt a sense of reverence for these authors who have died but will continue to be remembered through the ages.

Although the British Museum claims to be the most famous library in the world, and houses a large collection of the sculpture, ceramics, and paintings of numerous cultures, we were unable to spend enough time there to take in many of the wonders. However, we were able to spend some time in their very interesting manuscript room, where we saw original texts like *Beowulf*, the *Magna Carta, Paradise Lost,* and several others. We were captivated by this room and its documents. There was so much to see in London, and we vowed to return someday to continue our exploration of the museum.

Not to miss our usual shopping, we strolled Regent Street, where we merely window-shopped and found a few interesting stores in which to browse. Many stores were filled with luxuriously soft English wool clothing, and some imported fabrics and sweaters from Scotland. I was fascinated by this street, and as we were getting hungry, we decided to select a restaurant there.

At 233 Regent Street there was a restaurant called the Verreys, which was filled with English charm; most importantly, the food was delicious. At the time, I was a smoker and on the table was an ashtray with the restaurant's name, street, and logo on it. I thought it would be a great souvenir, and toyed with the idea of taking it. After dinner, I decided that it was a bad idea, and left the ashtray on the table.

As we were leaving, the receptionist handed me a beautifully wrapped package. You guessed it — the ashtray. I still get embarrassed telling the story. Was I glad I had left that ashtray on the table!! Bernie recently found that lovely ashtray stashed away with some old things in our garage. So much for necessary items; still, it brought back the old memory of an embarrassing moment, and now when I think of Regent Street, it is always that incident that is omnipresent.

One of the more fascinating aspects of London are its red double-decker buses; like all tourists, we loved these buses, and of course, the children wanted to ride on the upper deck. To be sure, the ride was a thrilling experience both for the kids and for us. British taxi cabs were another attraction that we loved. Both the cabs and the buses seemed to travel at breathtaking, unconscionable speeds, always maneuvering through the heavy traffic and ignoring pedestrians. Our thrill-seeking children enjoyed the reckless speed.

Again, like all tourists, we took one of our afternoon tours to see Big Ben, which overlooks the Thames River, and noticed that one could see and hear the clock from quite a distance. Another attraction was the Old Curiosity Shop on Portsmouth Street, a 17th century building believed to be the oldest shop in central London. Its uniqueness is its overhanging first floor that gives the rare impression of a London Streetscape from before the Great Fire of 1666.

All of those attractions paled in comparison to St. Paul's Cathedral, a building which has a dome comparable to that of St. Peter's in Rome. But what fascinated us was the whispering gallery, the unusual acoustics, and the mosaic ceiling in the dome. The nave, transepts, and choir are arranged in the shape of a cross. The church is Baroque in design, and is used for great ceremonial events, particular those for the monarchy.

Churches are omnipresent in London and All Hallows Church, another great cathedral, has Roman tiles in the crypt; it also had the unique distinction of hosting the marriage of John Quincy Adams in 1797, who later became a United States President. Though it was still beautiful, one could still see the effects of the Great Fire of 1666.

To our disappointment, our next planned attraction, the Tower of London, could not be seen; the line was simply too long. Thus, we had to leave London without seeing its amazing collection of jewels. We did see the Tower Bridge, however. There was so much to see and do in London that we could have used several more weeks; and we left promising to return.

Chapter 27

PARIS, FRANCE

Oh, *Paris!!* Our "around-the-world trip" was winding down. We were in Paris. Paris has many memorable and beautiful places and attractions to see, but what I remember most is how extraordinarily expensive everything was, just everything. We did lots of sightseeing along the Champs-Élysées. We spent hours in the Louvre admiring the many paintings, and we looked at Leonardo da Vinci's *Mona Lisa* from every conceivable angle — she still smiled. I could lose myself at the Louvre, which housed the sculpture of the *Venus de Milo* and other art. The Louvre is the largest museum and palace in the world, and houses more than 5,000 paintings.

If the Louvre was an absolutely must see, so, too, were the Cathedral of Notre Dame, a Gothic church, as well as the Sacré-Cœur Basilica. After the church visits, we went as far up as we could in the Eiffel Tower, and looked over much of beautiful Paris.

In the evening, we should have been tired, but we booked a night club tour to the Lido, a world famous night spot. This was for the two of us, and we allowed Brenda, age twelve, to babysit her brothers — not our standard procedure, but we were in a hotel in Paris and did not want to trust a stranger. The tour bus picked us up in front of our hotel; as we boarded the bus, to our surprise and amazement, there were Alice and Arthur Smith, our friends from New Jersey!

We were like ships passing in the night; we met for just a few brief moments, since they were taking a two-club tour and they departed at the next stop. We did, however, meet for coffee for a few minutes the following day. Needless to say, we spoke about the incidental meeting for years. Neither couple knew that the other was in Europe. The Smiths' daughter was at the Sorbonne, and they were visiting her. They had no idea we were traveling, and the meeting was coincidental, short, happy, and most unusual. The Japanese people on the bus did not know what to make of us and all the laughter, but I think they understood the coincidental meeting.

After a wonderful evening at the Lido, we returned to the hotel to find the doors locked — we had never heard of a hotel closing up! We banged and kicked until we got the desk clerk to open the doors. When we arrived in the children's room, Brenda had written a note: *"Mom and Dad, I stayed up until 12:10 and had to go to sleep."* What a night: first surprise, then thrill and excitement, then fright and pride in our daughter. She handled the situation well.

Another day came, and more sightseeing was on our agenda. We were on an excursion to Versailles, the Gardens and Palace of the Kings, the Hall of Mirrors, and the beautifully decorated apartments of the kings. The gardens were spectacularly beautiful and peaceful. We visited the Gallery of Battles and the Royal Chapel. I remember how privileged I felt to be exposed to all this history and splendor — we all did.

Despite all the beauty, magnificent buildings and broad avenues, the French still had outdoor public unisex toilets on the streets: they consisted of a concrete floor with a hole in the ground. Talk about culture shock! There seemed to be a dichotomy between the magnificence of Versailles and outdoor toilets, to say the least.

Brenda and Barbara in front of the Eiffel Tower; note the sweater and coat.

It was a cold summer day when Mark, Bernie, and Carl posed at the Eiffel Tower.

Chapter 28

MADRID, SPAIN

Each country had its unique attractions and its unusual cultural aspects, and Spain was no less so. It was August 6th when we arrived in Madrid, Spain, the next-to-last country on our round-the-world odyssey. It had truly been a journey of a lifetime!! So much history there and in every country that we could not absorb it all.

Our hotel was the Hotel Gran Via, on a street with a metropolitan spirit, lively with people, cafés, office buildings, and department stores. In Spain, we visited two towns, each special in its own way. In Madrid, a beautiful and cosmopolitan city, we spent hours in the Prado Museum, famous for its most exquisite paintings by Spanish masters El Greco, Velázquez, and Goya. Diego Velázquez' *The Maids of Honor* was one of my favorite paintings.

Among other notables housed in the Prado were the Italian and Flemish masters, Titian and Raphael, and modern painters such as Degas, Renoir, Manet, and numerous other world-famous artists. We had seen artwork by some of the greatest artists the world had ever known in the major European museums of the world, and we enjoyed all of them immensely. In Madrid, the Royal Library was another place of fascination, with its nineteen rooms, 200,000 volumes, and 6,000 manuscripts.

More importantly, Madrid was a beautiful city, with warm and friendly people. They were full of life during the early morning hours; however, they settled down for siesta at noon, and evening found them again full of life and happiness, ready to dine and dance. I loved their schedule and their vibrancy, their zest for life.

We were able to dine at a restaurant that featured flamenco dancers, and we thoroughly enjoyed the rapid dance and the click of the castanets. There we also learned that Spanish appetizers were called *tapas* and are much like the *puupuus* of Hawaii. Tapas could include calamara fritos, cured ham, meatballs, and olives. I loved the spirit of the people, their vitality and lifestyle.

Another city we visited in Spain was Toledo, one of the oldest cities in Europe. This city was El Greco's home; moreover, there was a cathedral that was built in the 11th century in the French Gothic style, which was majestic in appearance. Artwork and handicrafts abound in this area; their pottery and embroidered linens were outstanding. We saw the Alcázar, the fortress which was attacked during the Spanish Civil War; its ruins remain for visitors to see.

Portugal

Chapter 29

LISBON, PORTUGAL

Sadly, our last stop in Europe — Lisbon!! When we arrived in Lisbon, Portugal, on the 10th of August, we had been traveling for two months; we had left Kwajalein on the 15th of June. We were exhausted, but still excited and eager to see and learn. Lisbon is famous for many things, but one of its most important, of course, are the bull fights.

One afternoon, along with thousands of other tourists and natives, we attended one of these unusual events. There is much ceremony and ritual connected to a bull fight, and to the toreador and the matador, who are dressed in beautiful costumes and swathed in courage and bravery. We yelled *Olé!* with the crowd, understanding some, but not all, of the rituals. We were totally engaged and thrilled, but yelled with sorrow when the bull was injured. Fortunately, in Portugal bulls are not slain, and the toreador is seldom injured.

Noticeable, in Portugal, were the amount of glazed tiles used throughout the city, particularly the rooftops in the old city. Everywhere, murals were made of decorative tiles, which resulted in attractive, outstanding artwork along many of the streets.

The afternoon tour took us to Sintra and Estoril, where we visited castles and royal palaces; then the tour took us to the coastline, where long stretches of white sandy beaches met the azure blue water's edge. We saw the beautiful countryside where lush green cork trees grew, and we were told that two-thirds of the world's cork is produced in Portugal. The bountiful grape fields, reported to yield the best grapes for the world's best port wine, was the last part of the tour. This slower pace was a nice way to end our many days of excitement.

We were getting anxious now; it was hard to hold our attention. That night, although exhausted, Bernie and I managed another dinner for two late at night. We were in the land of Lancer's wine, and we did enjoy it.

Chapter 30

NY, HONOLULU, and NJ

And then, it was over, the journey that had altered our lives immeasurably forever. Thus, on August 12th, we arrived in New York, after circling JFK Airport for four hours; we delayed a welcome home party that my sister, Dorris and my brother-in-law, Gene, had arranged for us in Uniondale, New York. We simply needed time to rest; however, one cannot imagine how good it was see our family and friends. It was good to be on American soil. We had had an unbelievable journey — we had circled the globe! Nineteen countries in sixty-three days; we were happy and exhilarated, but exceedingly exhausted.

We returned to New Jersey for a couple of days, where Bernie had to report to RCA Moorestown. After such a trip, our hometown seemed quaint and quiet, yet still lovely as always. In New Jersey, we did not have much time to visit our friends, just a few days to take care of the house and to greet some of our closest friends. Mostly, we attempted to relax and bring our bodies and minds back into focus; after seeing so many fascinating sights that filled us with daily excitement, it is not easy to slow the body and mind. Indeed, we knew that our experiences would be with us for a lifetime, and that we welcomed.

Despite the momentary respite in Moorestown, we knew our travels would again start; on the 15th of August, we, the weary travelers, returned to Honolulu to await our ten-hour plane trip back to our island of paradise, Kwajalein. We had much to tell our friends, but we were happy to return to our daily routine and to our home.

Chapter 31

KWAJALEIN, HOME AGAIN

On the 18th of August, we were back where we started. It had been simply amazing, the things we had seen and done. We had exposed the children to the world, and by doing so, exposed them and ourselves to cultures vastly different from ours. Some were superior, others inferior, but each different in so many ways.

All of this added to our compassion and understanding of others in our universe; still, more importantly, the trip taught us to be greatly appreciative of our culture and country, however, different we were, however unjust in so many ways. Clearly, the Civil Rights Movement was a necessary element in our country; we all knew and understood that.

In our country, over the past years we had witnessed the assassination of three important people: our President, John F. Kennedy; our leading Civil Rights advocate, Dr. Martin Luther King, Jr.; and our President's brother, Attorney General Robert Kennedy. We had also witnessed great upheaval in our country: cities burning from Black unrest, and great and justified civil rights marches in the South — in Alabama, Arkansas, Mississippi, even in some northern cities. Yet, despite all these shortcomings and all these barriers to Blacks and other minorities, our own country seemed like a paradise compared to some of the third-world countries steeped in poverty and other human indignities. This was abundantly clear to all of us.

Thus, we had a greater empathy for the depressed peoples of Africa and some of the other underprivileged countries. It gave us a far greater empathy for others, plus taught us lessons that we will carry for the rest of our lives. This might be one of the reasons that Brenda chose to be a doctor and Mark chose to become an attorney, while Carl chose a profession in finance, all helping others in need: others who are far needier than they. Travelers are always changed and impacted by their journeys.

Back to reality and trailer number 505: it seemed like heaven. Tin City had never looked so good! We had a million slides to develop, a million stories to tell, and memories to last a lifetime. Kwajalein seemed different: still our peaceful paradise, but after all our enthusiasm for the Taj Mahal, the Pyramids, the Eiffel Tower, as to be expected, Kwajalein was somewhat of a deflation, almost as if air had been depressed from our bodies and our minds. But duty called, and we had to return to our daily routines: children in school, Bernie at work, and I at my other required duties and obligations.

We shared slides and experiences with many friends and neighbors. For weeks and months, our dinner table conversation turned to the world trip. Mark, always the analyst, stated: "White people should be careful; there are more dark people in the world than white." Profound for an eleven-year-old!

Chapter 32

BLACK REVOLUTION

We were in Moorestown when President John F. Kennedy was assassinated; we felt the deep impact and shared the grief and sorrow with the rest of the nation.

The march on Washington brought us new hope, and we were jubilant about the "I Have a Dream" speech by Dr. Martin Luther King, Jr. It became every Negroes dream, and particularly our dream. During the sixties, Dr. King stirred the conscience of the nation and caused us to look inward, and in doing so, changed the course of history. His nonviolent approach for justice had gathered momentum, and for his valiant efforts he was awarded the Nobel Prize for Peace.

We missed much of the Black Revolution while on Kwajalein; however, we were there when Dr. King was assassinated — what a sad time for all of us. I remember two people expressing their sorrow to me. I did not feel we were there to collect condolences for a fallen hero, however, he had changed the course of history, and yet to those on Kwajalein his death seemed a non-event. I remember leaving mass the Sunday following the assassination and asking the priest why he had not mentioned it in his homily. He looked blank, gave a slight shrug, and had no response. I thought this was a grievous omission. We shared this loss with no one but our family.

During those troubled times in the United States, we were enjoying peace, solitude, and island comfort; but we were consciously aware of the continued struggle of our race. In our absence, our race had gone from being *Negroes* to *Black*; from pressed, permed, or closely-cut hair to the naturally kinky curl and foot-high Afros; "Black Power!" had become a battle cry.

My Mother wrote that attitudes had changed and people seemed mean, unsmiling, and uncaring. This could be seen in every aspect of life. We missed all the changes and direct emotional involvement of the movement. However, we found that being a black professional in this island environment provided a platform for people to see a typical Black American family, not the imaginary negative image portrayed on television and in the papers.

We were ourselves, but we later found that being ourselves had allowed us to make a positive contribution to the movement. What they learned was simply that our aspirations, family values, goals, and ambitions for our children were the same as they had for their families — although we had to work harder to become successful because the playing field was never level, and never will be.

We understood that concept, since our children were introduced to racial injustice long before they arrived on Kwajalein. Kwajalein taught them that children could get along extremely well, operating under their own devices, without parental interference. That was proven in the Kwajalein Schools.

Brenda, always a strong personality, ran for President of the Student Council and won, despite the fact that she was challenged by four others, one of whom, oddly, was her brother. Sandy Trigg, another RCA daughter, was her campaign manager. Mark was his class's Council Representative, so he participated in making student law, and he was voted the best dancer in his class — we have yet to understand that one. Brenda was voted the most popular girl in her grade, and she was an Honor Roll student.

133

They were very much involved in all school activities. Because the children had been taught to accept all people and to believe themselves equal to all and inferior to none, they had a wonderful time on the island, and to this day they have diversity in their friends. They know exactly who they are, a lesson compounded on Kwajalein.

Chapter 33

MEXICO CITY VACATION

Although our world trip was over, we still enjoyed travel, and in the summer of 1969, we decided to vacation in Mexico City and Acapulco, a real two-week vacation. Of course, we had to return to New Jersey first, see the house and allow Bernie to report to RCA; then to New York to see our families. Our tenant, however, was long gone, taking with him an elaborate train set we had for the boys, but that is another story. All of this taken care of, we started our long-awaited trip to Mexico.

In Mexico City, we easily oriented ourselves in the beautiful, elegant, and comfortable Maria Isabela Hotel. The Sheraton Maria Isabela Hotel was one of Mexico City's grandest, situated on Paseo de la Reforma, a broad avenue that runs through the middle of the city, making points of interest very accessible. In fact, the inspiring Angel of Independence Monument, a national treasure, was right in front of the hotel. Moreover, the children loved the location and atmosphere; they were relaxed and enjoyed themselves; the employees seemed to cater to the children, and they loved all the attention and soaked it in. The family had a wonderful time.

We decided a sightseeing bus tour would be the best way to see some of this huge city, and we did indeed see many of the city's attractions; however, within three days, Bernie and I were hit by the high altitude and oxygen starvation, and we were aching and tired. Fortunately, the children were not affected.

Despite feeling ill, however, we were able to spend a Sunday in famous Chapultepec Park, the largest in Mexico City, frequented by Mexican families particularly on Sunday afternoons. Chapultepec Park has large flower gardens, a cactus garden, mini lakes for boating, a zoo, and shaded paths for strolling. It is no wonder that families spend so many pleasant hours enjoying the amenities of this park. Our children were able to observe games, some customs, and other activities of those families, plus have some interaction with Mexican children.

In addition, much to my joy, Mexico City was a shopper's paradise. Articles made of stone were everywhere: beautifully carved book ends, vases, and other novelties. Being a great shopper, I bought a white onyx pedestal fruit bowl that I carried on my lap all the way back to the island to ensure its safety. We saw bright Mexican pottery and lacquer-ware bowls made from gourds. However, my Mexican treasure was a papier-mâché nativity scene with figures twelve inches high, muted, but rich in color, which I purchased in a five-and-ten-cent store in the city. To this day, it is displayed proudly and reverently each year with our Christmas holiday decorations.

On one of our evenings, we took in a performance of the Mexican Folkloric dancers, observing the precision of the corps' steps and the magnificence of their costumes, vibrant in color and design. It was an outstanding show, startling and beautiful. After all of this, I don't think Mark will ever forgive us for not taking him to the Museum of Mexico City, but we had no energy for a museum tour. Our exhausted state caused Bernie and me to be anxious to leave.

TAXCO, MEXICO

From Mexico City, we were driven to the city of Taxco, located high in the rugged Sierra Madre mountains, where we spent one delightful night. Taxco is a little silver mining city much as it was in the 1500s, with narrow cobblestone streets and houses with red tile roofs, winding into the steep mountainside. It was like a true storybook — picturesque and beautiful. These sights would and did rival any of the magnificent scenes we had seen on our world travels.

It is hard to imagine the over 300 silver shops in this small city, crammed to overflowing with all kinds of jewelry: bracelets, earrings, and necklaces of the shiniest silver, some encrusted with turquoise, coral, and other gemstones. We could see the amazing workmanship displayed by these talented artisans, obviously generationally-passed talent. Taxco is known as the silver capital of the world, and best known for hand wrought silver. It is frequented by artists and tourists from around the world. We had dinner in the famous marketplace, where we enjoyed watching the artists with their easels and paints as they captured the city on canvas. It was absolutely magnificent.

It took four hours to drive from Taxco to Acapulco. We stopped once to see the Palace of Cortés, built by Hernándo Cortés, the Spanish conqueror of Mexico, which was 400 years old. We enjoyed the palace, the history depicted, and the artifacts displayed; the ride to Acapulco was scenic and smooth along a super highway.

ACAPULCO and LAS BRISAS

Finally, we were in beautiful, exotic Acapulco, where we stayed at Las Brisas, by far the most beautiful, posh hotel we have ever stayed in. Las Brisas was then and is now rated one of the ten best hotels in the world, and is known as the pink-and-white resort that offers private swimming pools with almost every room. Aptly named, its guest rooms were beautifully decorated in pink-and-white with simple elegance.

Furthermore, Las Brisas is also noted for its culinary excellence, graciousness, and ambience. Indeed, as such, we were pleasantly assured of excellent food, and, of course, we enjoyed delectable luncheons on the veranda serenaded by the strolling Mariachi Band. Las Brisas lived up to its reputation for culinary excellence, both for lunch and dinner.

To augment the theme, guests were provided pink-and-white jeeps to travel up and down the resort hills, as Las Brisas sits high up in the mountains overlooking Acapulco Bay, with a view that is breathtakingly beautiful. In addition, the jeeps provided another purpose: the waiters used them to deliver exotic, refreshing drinks and snacks to the guests. Watching the waiters drive up the hill, with one hand on the steering wheel, while the other hand balanced a tray of artfully presented tropical drinks, was a unique show unto itself. Not one beverage was wasted during our eight-day stay there.

Our accommodations were far above our ordinary expectations: we had two rooms and two private swimming pools, which the children used extensively — they used one pool in the morning and the other in the afternoon. No one enjoyed the pool more than Mark: we timed Mark one day — he stayed in the water for five hours without coming out to eat, which is his true passion.

Every day was spectacular and enjoyable, but one of our more splendid, enchanting, and enjoyable evenings was spent having dinner at the site of the La Quebrada Cliff Divers, which also served excellent food. The ambience of the restaurant was sophisticated, rugged, and Mexican. I was impressed with the décor: greenery jutted out of the rock walls of the La Perla restaurant. Equally impressive was the skill of La Quebrada Cliff Divers, who were truly daring. Obviously, only a skilled person could dive from such heights between the narrowest of rocks. Clearly an amazing and intriguing show, as well as dangerous.

Acapulco was a great place for relaxation, and we all enjoyed ourselves. We absorbed it all before our return to Honolulu. However, Montezuma's Revenge was beginning to consume us, even though we were using bottled water to brush our teeth and were careful about the eating of fresh vegetables and fruit. Still, this was affecting only Bernie and me — again, the children were spared. I decided it was the water in the beer. I stopped drinking the beer, and was healed almost immediately. Bernie did not believe me and continued to drink the beer, and he became weaker and weaker and thinner and thinner. We barely got him back to Honolulu to take him immediately to the Straub Clinic. He was only dehydrated; he was given medication and told to drink cranberry juice, and a cure would be imminent. Although weakened, Bernie was able to rest and regain some composure before our return to the island.

We were fortunate that our return to Honolulu was at a most historic time in space history: NASA had successfully landed a man on the moon, and we and the world were astounded. A man was actually on the moon! The *Honolulu Star-Bulletin* read on July 20, 1969, "Man's Most Exciting Day." The bald eagle was displayed landing on the moon with the symbol of *Apollo II,* and the faces of *Apollo II* Commander Neil Armstrong, Lieutenant Colonel Michael Collins, and Colonel Edwin "Buzz" Aldrin were proudly in focus.

The *Honolulu Advertiser*'s headline on July 21, 1969, screamed, "Man Walks on Moon!" An eight-page souvenir moon section was enclosed. The television and newspapers were filled with this extraordinary news, and we were so enthralled that we remained in our hotel room glued to the television; it was quite unusual for us to be in Honolulu and not gallivanting.

We were amazed, excited and overwhelmed by this technology, and the children and I leapt for joy and screamed with excitement. Bernie, the engineer, weakly acknowledged this engineering feat. I kept looking at the moon in disbelief. I think I really wanted to see a man or something on the moon to indicate that he was really there. I collected all the newspapers I could find for our historical files.

Clearly, 1969 had been an eventful year; however, when we returned to Kwajalein, summer activities were about to come to an end. School would soon resume; we would return to work, and the summer of 1969 would be over. What a marvelous summer it had been.

Chapter 34

A CULTURAL EXPERIENCE

I can truly say that one of my most memorable experiences on the island was the fellowship with the Marshallese women on a Saturday afternoon in September 1969. Seventy-five American women and eighty Marshallese women had a picnic on the Island of Carlos sponsored by the Protestant church.

As usual, the *Tarlang* was provided for our transportation. The food was supplied by the Americans, but more importantly, prepared by the Marshallese in their own custom. Holes were dug in the earth and fires started in these pits. Using coral rocks that had been washed and dried and heated until they were very hot, the Marshallese had their stove.

First, the chicken was marinated in soy sauce, then cooked over the hot stones on a rack covered with aluminum foil. I stood there, wondering what they had done before aluminum foil. To say the least, the chicken was delicious, of course, as were the rice balls — cooked rice rolled in fresh coconut. I do not care for sweet rice of any sort, but these were interesting and everyone seemed to enjoy them. In addition, they served something called "coconut apple" — the soft part of a coconut was ground into mush and poured into a cup, something similar to our Italian Ice.

For dishes, the Marshallese women tore off palm fronds and quickly wove them into trays that were used for plates. We were impressed by the adeptness with which this was accomplished. Needless to say, it was one of the most interesting days I had spent on the island. These women had shown us how they used the environment around them and used it successfully. We enjoyed watching them cook in their native way; more importantly, the fellowship we shared on the boat to Carlos and the bond of friendship we experienced that day will always be remembered; a delightful day with a more delightful people.

Chapter 35

LEAVING PARADISE

We were about to spend our final winter on Kwajalein. Lew Nelson, Bernie's manager from Moorestown, felt that a great assignment awaited Bernie if we would leave the summer of 1970. Extending his present assignment further would mean a seven-and-a-half year tour on Kwajalein. The children wanted to stay forever; however, Bernie and I thought Brenda should spend her four years of high school in Moorestown, and so, reluctantly, we prepared to leave our paradise.

It was hard to believe that we had been on the island for more than four years, four happy years away from quiet, staid, lovely Moorestown, and the unrest our race and nation had suffered in our absence. How would we readjust to life in the real world? The freedom we had enjoyed, a life almost free of prejudice, the beautiful spirit of the island, the friendly people, the marvelous warm weather, the blue skies, the sparkling Pacific, the excellent food, the long exotic rests and relaxations in the Hawaiian Islands, the Trouble Desk — all these wonderful experiences were soon to be only memories. God, I wanted to stay!!

The children did not want to leave Kwajalein; none of us really wanted to return stateside. But we still had the winter and spring to enjoy, and enjoy we did. I went on a rampage of acquiring any items I wanted to take home, and started planning the redecorating of our house in Moorestown, which lifted my spirits. We had far more to ship back than we had shipped out; it would be like Christmas in July when the boxes arrived in New Jersey.

While our island tour was almost over, we still planned a few side excursions before our return to our home in Moorestown. We invited Mother to Honolulu to show her some of the exciting places we had visited and enjoyed during our rest and relaxation periods. Obviously, Honolulu was itself a wonderful and exciting place to visit, and we wanted Mother to share the experience on our final visit.

Mother joined us in Oahu to see the sights and exciting places that had thrilled us. We took her to see Don Ho, the Hawaiian entertainer. We traveled again up the coastline for a closer look at Diamond Head, to Sea Life Park, the Punch Bowl, Pearl Harbor, the International Market Place, and finally, to a Hawaiian luau — all sights which we had enjoyed and wanted to share with her. Sadly, we bid a fond "Aloha" to Oahu, an island we were enamored of; we promised many future visits.

After our Hawaiian vacation, we made a long trip to California for a visit with our many friends; Mother visited with her nephew and his wife. California, like Hawaii, has numerous places of interest to see and visit; thus, we took Mother to Disneyland, Marineland, Knottsberry Farm, and Hollywood. Finally, we flew to Las Vegas — the bright lights of the strip, dinner clubs, and gambling casinos were all the absolute antithesis of the quiet, serene life on our Kwajalein paradise, and we loved it.

In Las Vegas, we had rooms at Caesar's Palace, a wonderful hotel. Romanesque in design, with a huge statue of Caesar standing tall in the courtyard as if to greet us, and surrounded by flowing fountains. We had a beautiful time, thoroughly enjoying the excitement and lights of the Las Vegas strip. We islanders were dazzled, for we had not seen so many bright lights in a very long time. The children went to their first nightclub, drank unlimited Cokes, and really felt grown-up, while we all enjoyed the Englebert Humperdink Show. At that time, he was an important and novel entertainer.

The following day, we left Las Vegas and drove to the Grand Canyon, up and around the North Rim, into Bryce Canyon and Zion National Park. The colors and depths of the canyons were spectacular, but I shall never forget the pink colors so distinct in Bryce Canyon. We gazed at Hoover Dam, with its awesome power and might.

After our return to Las Vegas, we bid tired Mother farewell as she boarded the plane to New York; we were not finished traveling, however, something we loved to do. We boarded a plane to Great Falls, Montana, rented a car, and drove first to Yellowstone National Park where we visited Old Faithful, and then to Glacier National Park.

Although it was June and the park was open, it was extremely cold, and our blood was thin from the higher altitude. There were warning signs to be aware of grizzly bears. We and a few Japanese tourists were the only people in the park. Our visit to the park was memorable only in that we were so extremely cold that we were forced to leave before we could enjoy the scenery, yet we knew that we would return someday at a warmer time.

Finally, it was inevitable: we had to return to Moorestown, New Jersey. Undoubtedly, and with great reason, we knew our lives would never be the same. The experiences we had had, the wonderful people, the exotic and beautiful places we had visited, the different cultures we had encountered, the lessons learned from a myriad of people — all of this permanently altered our vision.

What had truly delved into our hearts and minds was the warmth of the people of Kwajalein and similar places we visited; yet, in a greater sense, the uniqueness of the different cultures was also paramount to our vision. We learned to appreciate the differences we encountered; more importantly, we learned to appreciate the similarities. We were going home, our lives forever changed.

Chapter 36

AT HOME in MOORESTOWN

Four years after we returned to Moorestown, Brenda decided that medicine was her calling. We believed that her exposure to underprivileged people in the nations she witnessed subliminally influenced her choice of vocation.

Wellesley was her choice of college, and fortunately, she was accepted by that New England school. The entire family took her to school that fall. We readied her room and, knowing how much we would miss Brenda, we remained at the school, prolonging our stay into a ridiculous amount of time. Finally, it was their dinner hour; she and her assigned roommate departed for dinner, and we bade her goodbye. The last memory I had of Brenda was her walking toward the dining room with her partner, pushing up her glasses to wipe away the tears.

Four quiet, solemn people drove off the campus that evening. One would have thought we had buried her. No one spoke for several hours, and then Mark suggested we eat. We found a restaurant and stood in line for the hostess to assign us seats. She asked, "How many, please?" Bernie said, "Five," but our son Carl, said, "No, there are only four of us."

Brenda had prepared herself well in all her studies, but learning to speak French was all-important to her. She was determined to have command of a language other then English. Although she completed five years of French in high school, she also wanted to experience French in its native environs, and this she did by spending her sophomore Easter break in France with her teacher and classmates. But the summer of her junior year spent with a French family in Normandy, France, was most important; she cherishes that stay to this day. In that home, she was not allowed to speak English at all; because of this study, she was elevated to a higher level of French study at Wellesley.

Mark was a senior at Moorestown High and making applications to colleges; Carl was in eighth grade at the Middle School; Bernie, of course, was back in the Moorestown plant, while I was managing the One-Hour Martinizing Dry Cleaners we had opened in 1972. We were relatively content and at peace.

I believe it was late spring when Bernie came home with surprising and exciting news: Max Lehrer, Vice President of RCA, Moorestown, had requested that Bernie return to Kwajalein as RCA Site Manager. We were excited, but our first consideration was Carl. This would interrupt his high school years, as it would be a two-year assignment. The decision, we decided, should be Carl's.

We explained what it would mean to him and his father. After informing us that we were interrupting his athletic career, he decided it would benefit his father and was willing to make the sacrifice. He had not wanted to come home at all, but now he, too, had settled in. Brenda and Mark were excited about the prospect of our returning because they would be able to spend a few days in Honolulu and Christmas holidays on the island, since college students are permitted one island visit per year. Bernie accepted the assignment, and we were to be on the island by September of 1975.

Vice President Max Lehrer congratulates Bernie on his assignment as RCA Site Manager, Kwajalein, M.I.

Although it warmed the spirit to think of a second assignment, reality quickly imposed itself. What a logistical nightmare this was going to be!! Many of the things I had unpacked would have to be packed and shipped again. We now had experience in packing and shipping, plus we knew that entertaining would be a major part of this tour, so the good china, stemware, and silver were necessities, as were my favorite cookbooks.

And a logistical nightmare it was! I was sorting household goods and clothing for overseas; at the same time, I was getting Brenda ready to return to Wellesley for her sophomore year, and Mark was excitedly anticipating his freshman year at Syracuse, and we had loads of shopping to do for him. Shopping was a must for all of us.

Both students were to report to their respective schools at the same time. It was impossible to get Brenda to Massachusetts and Mark to New York without making Carl the sacrificial lamb again. He would be two weeks late for school on

Kwajalein, and he was starting high school; nonetheless, we began making plans to return to paradise, the unreal world of Kwajalein. The sparkling blue Pacific, the friendly people, the Trouble Desk, and, oh, the vacations in Hawaii. We were indeed returning to paradise!

We were like a gypsy caravan, with two cars packed to capacity driving to Massachusetts that summer day. Carl rode with Brenda, who was driving her father's car, which she was to use in our absence. Reaching Wellesley, we helped Brenda unload the car, but there was no time to help arrange her room. She was living alone this semester, so sharing was not a problem. We hugged, kissed, and said teary-eyed goodbyes. We had made arrangements with our friends, the Perhams, an RCA family temporarily located in the Boston area, to get her to the airport at Christmas time, and to keep her car until her return. Brenda had been their babysitter on Kwajalein, and there was a mutual love there. It is amazing how things can work out. Doug and Maryann were a blessing to us.

Our next stop was Syracuse University, to deposit Mark for his freshman year. He had a fine roommate named Dave Howlett; they have remained friends to this date. It was difficult leaving Mark and Brenda knowing we would be 6,000 miles away. Mark had little experience being away from his family: he had attended baseball camp for a week with his brother, and spent a week in Germany when his high school German class visited. We were leery because Syracuse is such a large school and Mark was only seventeen years old. We felt he would have been more comfortable in a smaller setting; we were right, but this was his choice, and he persevered and completed the four years, most of them with honors.

We made mental plans of how "Tour Two" could work for us. Our home would remain unoccupied for our use during the summers. Carl and I would return to Moorestown at the end of his school semester, while Brenda and Mark would join us when their semesters ended. Frankly, we hoped that they would find summer employment. Bernie would remain on Kwajalein until the latter part of the summer, then join us. Of course, he had to make his annual visit to RCA, and he was definitely needed to help take the college students to school. Thus, Bernie, Carl, and I returned to Moorestown to make the final preparations for our return to paradise.

Chapter 37

OUR RETURN to PARADISE

Honolulu was as beautiful as ever! We arrived at three-thirty in the afternoon on a Wednesday afternoon in September, 1975. We had a room on the 32nd floor of the Ala Moana Hotel, where we admired the fantastic view; by four o'clock in the afternoon, we were in the Ala Moana Shopping Center. We shopped the balance of Wednesday evening and all of Thursday. Since there were things that we needed and things that I wanted, I was thrilled, Bernie thought it a necessary evil, and Carl thought it a bore and a complete waste of time. Because we had a Friday flight to Kwajalein, there was only a short time to enjoy this beautiful city again and to obtain necessary supplies.

Sadly, we were no longer being transported by World Airway from Honolulu to Kwajalein, with all its delicious food and alcoholic beverages. Instead, the Military Air Command (MAC) was now our carrier. Oh, what a difference! The food was boxed, and there were no alcoholic beverages. Still, this did not bother me, but some of our colleagues thought it several steps down from our usual luxury. Needless to say, since we were traveling on a big cargo plane reminiscent of what we had seen in the movies, they were correct. What bothered me most was that my feet were cold from Honolulu to Kwajalein, a ten-hour flight, even though I had them wrapped in a blanket. The thought occurred to me that I would not be running back and forth to Honolulu as often as I had before — not in this kind of plane. However, the MAC flight got us there safely and that was all that mattered.

There was an unbelievable welcoming committee to greet us. Beautiful leis were placed around our necks; it was a

151

royal welcome in every way. Jim Caskey, RCA Service Company Site Manager, and his wife, Jo, and Pauline and Bill Clark, long time friends, were our sponsors, and they had taken care of every detail. Some of Carl's friends who had never left the island were there to greet him, and he immediately left us and was again comfortable and happy in his surroundings.

Jo and Jim Caskey had prepared a delectable lunch of chicken salad and an orange mold containing pineapple and pecans, which she served at her home. Jo had stocked our refrigerator with beverages and an assortment of breakfast foods: we could not have asked for more. Later that evening, we dined with the Caskeys and Clarks, a meal of lasagna with all the trimmings, a delightful dinner and reunion; however, jet lag overcame us, and we had to ask to be excused early.

On Saturday night, our new life of all the entertaining and being entertained began, with a party with a Hawaiian theme that the Clarks hosted for us on their large patio. One could feel the island breezes that flickered the many tiki torches surrounding the patio. In addition, all the guests were dressed in bright muumuus and aloha shirts.

The food was exquisite; we dined on a menu of cranberry salad mold, baked ham, turkey, stuffing, sweet potatoes, and green peas; the desserts were pecan and blueberry pies. All of this delicious food was preceded by a large assortment of puupuus and cocktails. Although the food was delicious, we were most happy to see many of our old friends, some of whom had never left the island, others who were returnees, and some who were new introductions. The party was fabulous! The sponsors and guests were fantastic, and we were happy to be back.

Since my husband was Site Manager on this assignment, the parties continued. Indeed, the parties were nonstop. A party at the Officers' Club was held to introduce me to the wives of the staff and military. The Site Manager for MIT and his wife, Dr. and Mrs. Pippert, had cocktails and dinner for us at their quarters; the RCA staff also held a cocktail party in our honor on the patio of William Sandkuhler, the RCA Logistics Manager and his wife, Maureen. We were wined and dined by everyone. I was impressed and really made to feel welcome, different from the last stay, but no less warm and friendly.

The new Site Manager and wife are greeted by the military

Finally, it was time to start working on our quarters. The ultimate in living on the island was, of course, the big house — and we were now the tenants of the house.

The RCA Site Manager's house, Kwajalein: our only piece
of ocean-front property, and we loved it

The living room and dining room were together, large, and spacious. There was a large bookcase in the living room area that had been previously used as a room divider, but I decided it would better serve our needs as a place for our stereo equipment, books, and artifacts. The living room was large enough for three conversational groupings, so I visited the Furniture Warehouse and was successful in acquiring matching pieces to complete the groupings.

Danish-style furniture upholstered in electric blue was available, and the carpet was the color of eggplant. I had purchased white batiste drapes stateside for the living room and dining room windows; I had had measurements sent to me, and batiste was a perfect choice. With the drapes closed, one could see silhouettes of swaying palms in the front, and palms and breaking ocean in the back; open, and it was heaven! I continued to work on making our island home lovely and comfortable. Finally, it was a beautifully decorated house, and we enjoyed living there. I even had a potted palm tree growing in the living room!

The house was on a large corner lot very close to the ocean, my only piece of ocean-front property and we loved it. The ocean air played havoc with the metal roof on the patio, and it had to be replaced. Bernie painted the patio floor and bar, and we placed large potted plants around and hung colorful patio lights; thus, the outside became an exciting addition to the house. I considered the house and patio perfect for our comfort and entertaining.

At night, when the lights were out, little sea creatures were our uninvited patio guests. They crawled up from the ocean and invited themselves to inspect the premises. Often, I would scoop them up and place them in the freezer; after freezing, I allowed them to thaw, cleaned them, and added them to my shell collection. My shell collection grew by leaps and bounds on that ocean property.

Chapter 38

CHRISTMAS KWAJALEIN-STYLE
and the ACCIDENT

The holiday parties were in full swing. I was decorating the house for Christmas, baking, cooking, and freezing in the true holiday tradition. I wanted this Christmas to be especially wonderful for all the Darrells, since this was to be our first Christmas in the big house. Brenda and Mark were coming from college, and we were ecstatic!!

Despite all our happiness and anticipation for this holiday season, when we were attending a holiday party, the joyous spirit was broken. Ominously, we received a call from the hospital that Carl had been injured, and we left immediately and biked to the hospital. Though we were hopeful, Carl was in very serious condition. Dr. Beal stated in no uncertain terms: "In two more minutes, his life would have been over."

Carl, like so many young people, had been leaving the Teen Center when he decided to take a trial run on a friend's bike. The bike was abnormally constructed, as are many of the Kwaj bikes; this is what attracted his attention. The bike was difficult to manage, and he proceeded cautiously into the street and back. As he approached the building, he applied the brakes, but they failed. Unable to dismount, he had used his leg to ward off the impact, and his leg shattered the window, resulting in multiple lacerations. Had he not used his leg, he would have been decapitated.

Only the astute actions of Dave White, Director of the Teen Center, and Bob Ford, Coordinator of Pools and Beaches, saved his life. They knew and used the proper techniques for applying pressure to the strategic points to slow the flow of blood. Fortunately for us, Kwajalein hospital kept a list of residents' blood types on file, and they called on them as needed. At the time of the accident, one pint of blood was supplied by his father, and one pint was supplied by Rudy Hergenrother, a Sylvania manager; there was no wait for typing.

Dr. Beal primarily put Carl's leg back together; it took over three-and-a-half hours to sew the muscles and tendons together. Only God brought him through such an ordeal with no temperature over 100°, no infection, nor any other impediment to success. After the swelling subsided, his leg was placed in cast to keep the leg immobile and hold his foot straight. Four to six weeks would tell the story of his future, when the Straub Clinic, in Honolulu, would give their decision.

Dr. Beal and his staff did a miraculous job. We praised him and the entire Kwajalein staff in person and to the press. Their work was prompt, precise, and efficient, and we will forever be grateful to them. When we had time to breathe, we looked in the hospital corridor; it was filled with the guests from the party that was so abruptly disrupted. Sixteen friends surrounded Bernie and me, encouraging us and praying for Carl. They stayed until Carl was wheeled from the operating room. We will forever believe that the prayers of the Kwajalein community brought Carl through the most trying time of his life and ours.

All of Carl's friends gave enormous support and spent time comforting and encouraging him. The community was outstanding, but the children were simply amazing!! How do you celebrate Christmas so soon after your child has almost died? We did it by giving thanks to God that he was still alive!! Our faith took over, and we had nothing but thanksgiving for the miracle that Carl was spared. I told him that his life was spared for some purpose, so he had better make something good of his life — he owed God one.

157

The advance Christmas preparation was now helpful, as I was spending so much time at the hospital. Because we did not want to spoil Brenda and Mark's Christmas travels, we had not told them about the accident. They were already having panic attacks because of the impending United Airlines strike, plus we did not want to spoil their excitement for an island Christmas. Mark had to eventually leave New York from Rochester, thanks to the Howletts, and Brenda left Boston, thanks to the Perhams.

The two met in Denver and rode first class (the only seats available, or so they told us) from there to Honolulu. They had a great time en route, and were all smiles when we greeted them, then looked around and asked, "Where is Carl?" This was difficult. When we told them, Brenda went into hysterical laughter, and Mark was stunned into silence. We went to the hospital to see Carl and I cannot explain the mixture of emotions in that room.

Carl was with us Christmas Day because an ambulance brought him home at eleven o'clock to be with us; a corpsman came at two o'clock to administer his antibiotic shot, and at five o'clock they came to return him to the hospital. The following day he was released, still wearing a cast and using crutches, but we were all together on Christmas Day, and there was nothing we loved better. Though Carl's condition was foremost in our thoughts, the holidays were wonderful: we enjoyed our first Christmas in the island house, and we were grateful for the spirit of the season.

The young people had many activities, particularly the college students, who had numerous reunions and great activities. Although Carl was a spectator for the first time and could not enjoy the physical activities, we were all happy to be on the island together; in fact, there was no one unhappy on our little bit of paradise.

Kwajalein's school resumed while our children were still on break. Mark helped Carl get to school for a couple of days until his departure, then Carl made it on his own. He did a great job of keeping up, but he had to make the mental adjustment of not participating in sports, something he greatly loved. Brenda's school break was so long that she actually took a job on Roi-Namur after everyone else had departed. She was thrilled to fly to work with her father every day, performing a clerical job.

With the school breaks over, there was a quiet stillness over the island. After all of the hustle and bustle of preparing for the young people's arrival, they had departed, taking with them the joyous laughter and the energy that only the young can produce. The sounds of music and dancing returned to the norm; there were fewer bicycles on the road and fewer groups of young people talking and laughing as they utilized the taxi service. In our house, the telephones seemed to have stopped ringing and there were no more doors slammed: it was too quiet; we missed the children, and their gaiety and spontaneity.

With the holidays over, it was time to visit the best Orthopedic Specialist at Straub Clinic in Honolulu to further evaluate Carl's leg, so we embarked on our medical journey. We had a warm sendoff the morning we departed; the Kwajites were there offering prayers, and advised that we not allow anything artificial be placed in his leg. They all insisted that nature had a way of healing itself, if allowed. That was sound advice; the Straub Orthopedic team agreed, and they determined that Carl's hospital stay would be from eight to ten days. However, the subsequent surgery revealed that there was no glass or nerve damage, nor was there a blocked artery, and no other surgery was necessary. God was still with us.

Bernie returned to Kwajalein to his job, and I stayed with Carl until his discharge. His leg was closed and he was given this advice: if he lived a clean life, with no alcohol or tobacco, he should have success with his leg. With the cast replaced, he was given a physical therapy regimen. A host of friends were at the airport to welcome him back, and he returned to school and used his leg as much as possible. Wearing the cast caused a multiplicity of blisters, which resulted in an infection that impeded the therapeutic process. Someone suggested we discontinue the use of the medicated cleanser and cleanse his heel with plain water. This was the solution, and in about a week we noticed the healing process had begun.

Geckos are prevalent on the island, and occasionally they would become house guests. One night after Carl returned home, we heard him scream, and ran quickly to his room to find that a gecko had somehow invaded his cast. It took about fifteen minutes to gently shake the leg and poke around inside the cast to remove the intruder. After its successful removal, we all laughed and decided that soon this nightmare would be over and behind us.

Carl truly displayed his stamina during this ordeal; indeed, he was magnificent. He took all the discomfort in his stride: he had strong determination, was courageous, always hopeful, and yet kept his sense of humor. Although he missed many days in the classroom, his schoolwork never suffered. He was a fourteen year old to be admired, and we surely admired his attitude and courage.

We had one more trip to Straub, to see Dr. Linborn to have the cast removed, and we took the long flight knowing that good news would await us. After the cast removal and examination, we were given the okay to return to Kwajalein. Walking without the cast for the first time, Carl walked with great lightness and resiliency. He had conquered another major obstacle.

By the month of March, Carl was wearing a shoe, and was encouraged to resume bike riding; eventually, he resumed tennis. His first tennis match was thrilling to those in attendance; everyone was so grateful for his return. But for me, the greatest proof of his recovery was when he donned his surfer bathing suit and tennis shorts, revealing that horrendous scar that zigzagged from his upper thigh to the calf of his leg, and headed for the swimming pool. He was neither ashamed nor self-conscious; he was undaunted.

I was so proud of him, and, I might add, the girls still adored him. We were so elated that he was on his way back; it appeared that the physical and emotional strain were behind Carl, as well as for the rest of the family. Eventually, he regained ninety percent of his leg's mobility. He walks with a slight limp, but it is the scar that is the constant reminder of how much he was blessed.

Chapter 39

ISLAND CHANGES and the PARTY

The MAC flight was not the only change noticed on our return. Our greatest surprise — to my disappointment, television had come to Kwajalein. This was not welcomed by me or many of our friends. My children read incessantly on Tour One; Brenda and Mark devoured books. A memorable moment for me was seeing Brenda and four or five of her friends lying horizontally on her bed, feet against the wall, reading and swapping books as they completed them. Reading had become a welcome change when we first arrived on island: it had replaced stateside TV, but now that was over. The television transmitter emanated from the island of Ebeye.

However, a welcome, necessary change was the introduction of long-distance telephones. With two children in the States, this was a heartwarming bit of news, and a major improvement. No more trying to remember to say "over" with the radio patch, something neither my mother nor I ever really conquered, although our friend, Bob Ray, will always be remembered for his endurance while we tried to get it right, enabling us to greet Mother and family on holidays.

Another major change was the emergence of "Silver City" in our five-year absence: silver trailers had been brought in to accommodate the increased island population. Since they were placed at the northern end of the island, off Emon Beach, void of trees and shrubbery and swaying palms, the area was dubbed, "Silver City." The trailers glistened in the sunshine, the light of this barren area. In addition, some garden-type homes had been erected for the Marshallese on Ebeye, giving them substantial roofs and more living space. This was a welcomed and ongoing project.

Eventually, our major entertainment event for 1975 was about to take place. About six months after our return to the island, Max Lehrer, Vice President of RCA, Ted Lewis, Manager of the PRESS Program, and Bill Givens, RCA Service Company Vice President, and members of his team were to make their first visit to Kwajalein with Bernie as Site Manager. This generated excitement for us because we wanted them to see that we were handling the job well.

After we received their agenda, we went into full gear with plans to execute a perfect weekend visit. Obviously, I began to peruse my cookbooks in search of delectable menus because if ever one wanted to put a best foot forward, it was now. Max wanted to visit Roi-Namur on Friday afternoon to see the radar site. As customary, he would meet with the military brass and company representatives. We wanted to welcome him in the warmest manner, make him comfortable, and let him know that we were pleased that he had selected Bernie for the job.

Several activities were planned, including a lunch at our quarters, which would enable them to spend the balance of the afternoon on Roi-Namur, and finally, an evening cocktail party at the Yukwe Yuk, the Officers' Club, which would include all heads of the companies, their wives, the military command and their spouses, and all RCA personnel and their wives.

Because I considered Mary Murakami, an RCA wife, an excellent arranger of tropical flowers, I enlisted her assistance, and she consented to make all the arrangements for our home and the club. Since flowers are limited on Kwajalein, I arranged to have flowers flown in from Oahu, Hawaii: anthuriums, birds-of-paradise, ginger, ti leaves, and other tropical flowers to create an aloha atmosphere.

These occasions are always festive, with women wearing long colorful muumuus and the men usually wearing island

163

print shirts. So much of Kwajalein Island life was inspired by Hawaii, and the food was no exception, particularly the heavy puupuus. Since the hors d'œuvres were substantial, they often replaced dinner. Because of the enormity and importance of the occasion, the Officers' Club prepared the suggested menu: trays of iced shrimp, meatballs, beef with rolls, crab puffs, deviled eggs, salads, egg rolls, and teriyaki beef, all of which were beautifully displayed on tiered buffet tables.

In addition, the tropical flowers, the ladies and men adorned in colorful party attire, all combined to make a delightful island picture. We arranged an informal receiving line to make sure Max and the RCA entourage were introduced to everyone.

Accordingly, dinner for our stateside guests was held at our home with the staff members and their wives. We had informed our maid that the big, big, boss from the States was coming and the house had to be immaculate. By now, she knew what "spit and polish" meant, and she did an outstanding job; we were ready to welcome our distinguished guests.

First, hors d'œuvres and drinks were served on the patio, where the roar of the ocean mingled with the warm island breezes, creating an idyllic atmosphere for the occasion; then we moved inside for dinner. For dinner, I had decided on a vegetable salad and an entrée of beef tenderloin stuffed with lobster tail; a fluffy white potato casserole topped with crispy fried onion rings; and broccoli and carrots completed the meal. Our dessert, which was marble cake, was served with coffee, then after dinner drinks followed.

Needless to say, there was much story telling and good conversation, since many of us had not seen our boss for quite sometime. Everything was delightful — the food, the ambience, and the people. Above all else, Max paid me the highest compliment, when he stated that he knew what he had in Bernie, but Barbara was a bonus. However much we had enjoyed Max and Ted and our Service Company guests, they had enjoyed it even more: the thank-you notes we received were glowing and full of praise. I still smile when I think of those few days and the preparations we made for success, and the enjoyment we had in our guests.

SUMMER in MOORESTOWN

In the late spring of 1976, Carl and I returned to our home in Moorestown; Brenda and Mark soon followed, and things worked out as planned. They both obtained summer employment at RCA, part of their summer program for students. To add joy to the summer, two of Brenda's classmates from Wellesley were going to Africa to do a work/study program for the summer, and at Brenda's request, we hosted a party for them.

This party was held in our yard, and young people came from Washington, DC; Baltimore, Maryland; New York, New York; Philadelphia, Pennsylvania; and Boston and Wellesley, Massachusetts. The word had really spread that a party was going to happen. I had engaged the services of neighbors to help keep all under control, but happily, that was not necessary. More than 100 people were there having good clean fun. At times, the music became too loud, but that was immediately corrected. The rules and regulations had been established before the party began, and my children knew they had to adhere to those rules. We were happy to have given those two young ladies a wonderful sendoff for their work/studies in Africa.

As summer ended, Bernie returned, and Brenda and Mark retired from their summer employment and we did the back-to-school routine. By now, we had polished the routine to a science; still, departure is always difficult. Bernie, Carl, and I returned to Honolulu and then Kwajalein. As usual, I had a little shopping to do, but fortunately, most of it had been accomplished in New Jersey. We were starting our second year of this tour, but were soon to find out that it would not be the final year.

Chapter 40

KWAJALEIN, SECOND YEAR
of TOUR II

Bernie and I continued to host luncheons and dinner parties as required, or made arrangements for others to host families. Hail and farewell parties were important to the RCA family, and most were quite impressive no matter who hosted them. Hosting dinner parties and luncheons was always a pleasure for me, and I think this may be where I developed the love of entertaining in this manner. At least I had lots of practice on Kwajalein.

Brenda and Mark, as well as other college students were looking forward to spending their winter vacation in Honolulu and Kwajalein Island in the Pacific. Although many events would be held during this Christmas, it was a deep sea fishing trip planned by Mr. William Sandkuhler, RCA's Logistic Administrator, that was the highlight of the season — and what an exciting fishing trip it was!!

Carl Vincent opted not to attend, since fishing was too slow for him. Nevertheless, Brenda and Mark and others students had the time of their lives. Sea sickness was not a problem for them, and Mark proudly came home with a tuna as long as he; not to be outdistanced, Brenda had a tuna equally as large. Obviously, we did not know what to do with all the fish. Leave it to Bernie, who promptly decided the best place to clean the fish was our bathtub. He washed and dissected those fish, seemingly for hours. Finally, he had cut it into serving pieces, and we wrapped it all for the freezers.

Our friends and neighbors were elated: we had tuna for everyone. At the end of this activity, I had to make our bathroom suitable for human use again; with a lot of scrubbing, rinsing, and deodorizing, the tremendous job was accomplished. Although the students had a wonderful time attending many events, the fishing trip was the hit of the season. It was a winter holiday to be long remembered.

A THIRD YEAR

By now, we had learned this was not to be our last Christmas on this island of paradise. Ted Lewis, manager of PRESS, and MIT management had recommended Bernie continue on as Site Manager, and Max Lehrer, RCA Vice President, concurred.

A three-year term as Site Manager was unusual, as a Site Manager's tour is two years. The children were delighted, even Carl, who would now spend only his senior year at Moorestown High School. I, who never stopped loving Kwajalein, found it an easy addition, and Bernie was already comfortable in his position.

Life proceeded as usual until we readied for our summer departure. Carl and I opened the house in Moorestown, and waited for Mark and Brenda's arrival. Greeting friends and neighbors was always a pleasure, and as before, summer employment was found by our college students. Summer entailed being with friends and family, and shopping for the return to school. Somehow the time passed quickly, and soon we awaited Bernie's arrival, to visit and assist with the departure and the return to the colleges.

For the three of us, it was a return to paradise, with our usual stopover in Hawaii. Hawaii is always a pleasure to visit; no matter how many times we arrive, it is always exhilarating — it simply makes my spirit soar. This arrival was no exception, and Bernie, Carl, and I checked into the Marriott

Hotel, relaxed, and enjoyed the island for a couple of days before our return to Kwajalein.

The first major event of the fall season was an anniversary party for Bernie and me. On October 5th, 1977, Bernie and I would celebrate our 25th wedding anniversary. While we were contemplating how we would celebrate this significant occasion on the small island, our friends Elinor and Carmillo Vitullo had planned a party in our honor on their patio. It was a beautiful party, with all the island atmosphere, food, and gaiety; we were so pleasantly surprised.

An added joy, was the gift that all our RCA family presented to us — a Waterford decanter with a silver throat that had been engraved to commemorate the occasion. Our 25th anniversary was remembered in fine style; additionally, my favorite saleslady at Macy's encouraged Bernie to buy me pair of Waterford crystal candelabras as a gift. They would not have been my choice, but I was told to put them on the table and see what happened. Well, I fell in love with them, and they are still a treasure these twenty-seven years later.

After all the wonderful years on the island for the children and for us, December 1977 was truly to be our children's last island visit. They had had three wonderful winter vacations, filled with happiness and wonderful memories among friends never to be forgotten. I had prepared all of our holiday foods, the house was well decorated, and we thoroughly enjoyed the season. We took pictures of everyone, singularly and together, in front of the Christmas tree and amid the decorations. We were going to have pictures to cherish forever. It was after the children had departed that Bernie realized he had failed to put film in the camera; all of our posing was for naught. I became hopeful that our holiday joy was so deeply embedded in our hearts and minds that the memories would never fade.

As our three-year period was almost over, the farewell parties began, and we were feted at our departure as we had been upon arrival. There was the formal farewell for the Site Manager; in addition, the women had a party at Emon Beach with the theme of the Boardwalk of Atlantic City, a charming send off for me, and many individuals hosted us.

Then the packing out process had to begin: essentials were flown home, and the remaining household goods were sent by boat. However, all household goods had to clear customs upon arrival stateside. I began to reflect on the events of the past three years: the many happy times, the disappointments, and the heartbreak. There was so much to remember — the dinner parties, large and small; luncheons; golf tournaments; sailing races; picnics on Roi-Namur and Carlos Islands; the carnivals; re-entry of missiles; scrubbed missions; Christmas expectations and joy; medical trips to the Straub Clinic; trips to Hawaii; and the never to be forgotten, gentle Marshallese people. These special and unique memories can never be eradicated.

However much we enjoyed Kwajalein, its people, and its culture, our second tour proved prophetic. My Mother had been quite unhappy that we chose a return tour, and stated clearly what later would become prophetic — that we were pushing our luck. She thought that one successful tour could not be repeated.

Needless to say, she was correct in some aspects. Several unhappy incidents occurred: Carl's accident was by far the most devastating; the following year, Bernie had to leave the island for a week's stay at the Straub Clinic; and most heart-wrenching for me was that he had to go alone while I stayed behind with Carl. However, the goodness of most of the people never ceased to amaze me. While Bernie was in the clinic, a Kwajalein telephone operator would place a call to the clinic for me each morning so that I would have the comfort of knowing he rested well and was on the way to recovery. He returned to the island fully recovered and ready to resume work.

Similarly, another almost mishap occurred when a co-worker and I were departing from the island of Ebeye, after completing a volunteer job for the native islanders. A water taxi was our mode of transportation, and when we were halfway home, the boat sprang a leak. I looked at my co-worker, then we both looked at the boat operator. He began to bail water, and we grabbed pails and assisted. I looked at all the water in that little boat, and all the water surrounding us, and all I could think was that my Mother had told me not to come back here. Since the pilot was unable to stop the leak, we bailed water all the way back to Kwajalein, thanking God for a safe, though eventful, return.

Undoubtedly, nothing could be more horrific than receiving a telephone call that your house has had a fire when you are 6,000 miles from home. The phone call shocked us into reality. We were in the midst of the fall season when the call came from our neighbors and friends, Barbara and Cephas Green, stating there had been a fire at our home. Cephas, in his inimitable fashion, stated that he was standing in our living room looking up at the sky.

This was horrifying, very unsettling news, and there was nothing we could do except rely on friends and family. How had it happened, we did not know; although Brenda and three friends had been at the house for the weekend, none of the girls smoked. After their departure, however, neighbors from across the street noticed smoke from the roof and called the Fire Department and the Greens, because they knew that the Greens had the keys to the premises and the information on our whereabouts.

There is nothing like having good friends, neighbors, and family at such a critical time. According to the Fire Department, squirrels had entered the rafters and gnawed electric wires, which caused a short and resulted in the fire. Fortunately, there was not enormous damage; the contractor who had just added an addition to our house was called and he took care of the repairs. Jack, Bernie's youngest brother, came down from New York to oversee the repairs, the painting, and smoke odor removal; happily, we did not have to return home.

Ted Lewis, one of Bernie's RCA Managers at Moorestown, went to the house so he could reassure us that all was well and we need not return to New Jersey. In fact, when we returned the following summer, there was no indication that anything so dire had occurred. If we had not returned for a second tour, then these incidents might not have occurred. Who knows? Perhaps life is preordained.

We had lived in the Marshall Islands for almost eight years. It is difficult to recount all the benefits derived from this experience. Travel, of course, was a major benefit; the exposure and the eventual enhancement of our world view cannot be measured. The seed to explore had been planted, and our children and grandchildren will continue to cultivate the seed.

We had begun to think of the world as a neighborhood, shrinking in size, causing us to feel a closeness and understanding of other races and cultures. Heightened empathy for the needs of others was also a major part of that development. A major plus was the comfort we felt when associating with all kinds of people. In our first four years, we were on the engineering level, and on the second tour we had to associate with the heads of companies and top military brass, but we were able to handle both associations happily and easily.

One can imagine our sorrow and sadness at these farewell parties. The joy of entertaining, the hail and farewell parties, the gaiety and the heartbreak had come to an end, and we had to say a final goodbye to our island paradise and re-enter the real world.

However much we would miss the island of paradise, we had so much to look forward to. Brenda was graduating from Wellesley College the weekend of May 26th, 1978, a day we had long awaited, and all the family planned to be there, including the grandparents and an aunt. Mark would graduate from Syracuse University in the spring, and would take the LSAT in pursuit of law school, and Carl would complete his senior year at Moorestown High School. I would put our home in order and look for another job, and Bernie would return to his new challenge at the Moorestown plant.

We had enjoyed this idyllic island, the house, the people, the work, and the entire Kwajalein experience so much, and it was extremely difficult to leave. But leave we must; after all, our other life awaited, and that, too, was desirable. It would be good to be closer to family and reconnect with friends and organizations. A wide world awaited us, offering theatres, museums, planetariums, shopping malls, and the real Macy's. I think we were ready.

VACATION/MOORESTOWN

Before arriving at our home in Moorestown, however, Bernie, Carl, and I had planned a vacation on the way home, to include several days on Oahu, then on to the Marriott on Maui, and finally to Lake Tahoe, Nevada. As usual, we enjoyed the islands, then bade them farewell and boarded the plane to Lake Tahoe. Our accommodations were at Harrah's, and exquisite accommodations they were.

We had been told to check our golf clubs as they were not allowed in the rooms. When we entered the suite, we could understand why: the rooms were mirrored from floor to ceiling, and tastefully decorated with a modern flair, including a bathroom with plush white bathmats, a sizable TV, and telephones.

After enjoying all the luxurious accommodations, the casinos, and the nightclubs, the Sierra Nevada mountain range, and the crystal clear lake, we were ready to depart. We arrived at the outdoor airport and were waiting for our plane, enjoying the mountain view, when something unusual happened — snow began to fall, and it continued to fall heavily until there was a complete whiteout; the mountains disappeared before our eyes.

Snow quickly blanketed the town; one would not have known that mountains ever existed there. This was a fierce snowstorm, and we were told that no planes would be arriving or departing. At first, we were amazed, then stunned; then, we became cognizant that we had to make some other plans to depart Lake Tahoe. Realizing it was a short distance to Reno, we rented a car and began our drive to Reno.

Although we knew Reno had a history worth discovering, we had no time to sightsee, no time for new discoveries: Brenda was graduating from college, and we were homeward bound. We departed Nevada from Reno, now the last leg of our journey.

We were leaving behind a world that had truly awakened and enriched our lives, added layers of depth to our compassion and vision, and given us indelible memories that will surely last a lifetime.

EPILOGUE:

THE TRAVELS CONTINUE —
the ORIENT EXPRESS and EUROPE

Several years later, after we had settled into our home in Moorestown and had survived the many graduations, the thought of celebrating our 40th wedding anniversary became paramount in our minds. We decided a five-week sojourn to Europe would be a meaningful way to celebrate this special occasion, because it had been our desire to spend some time in the Swiss and French Alps.

Our plan was to spend a week each in London, the Netherlands, France, Spain, and Switzerland. Because of these plans, our children decided to give us a trip on the Orient Express, and what excitement that generated. Happily, we altered our established schedule to include the fabulous train trip. Since the Orient Express departed from Zurich, Switzerland, we had to adjust our itinerary to allow one day in Zurich at the outset, and depart from that hotel to the train station.

We arrived at the train as advised, dressed for the evening. I was wearing a red sequined blouse with black silk pants, while Bernie's attire was black tie. On the platform were fellow travelers dressed in fancy clothes, reminiscent of the Roaring Twenties, and dancing to twenties music in preparation for a grand evening. We were greeted by a uniformed attendant stating in a beautiful accent: "Mr. and Mrs. Darrell, we have been waiting for you." Elegance personified!!

We were promptly relieved of our luggage and directed to our compartment, a rather small teak-paneled room, and then to our table in the dining room. In the dining room, more travelers were attired in roaring twenties outfits, and the atmosphere was electric. I quickly surveyed the entire dining room, then focused on the small, colorful fringed lamp on our table, noticing they adorned all the tables. The dining room was quiet elegance in its décor, filled with the quiet happiness of the travelers.

Although I cannot remember what we dined on, I do remember it was outstanding and we had impeccable service. We loved the ambience of the evening, but as night had fallen, there was no sightseeing as the train roared toward Paris. After enjoying our first evening on the Orient Express, we retired to our room to find that the bunk beds had been prepared for us with bed linens made of the most luxurious damask.

To my astonishment, the bathroom had no shower; I had to transport myself back in time and realize that in that era, accommodations had been smaller and modern plumbing not so prevalent. What the compartment lacked in space, it made up for in elegance. The bathroom had teak walls, and the sink was white porcelain with pink roses in the design, with porcelain fixtures and the fluffiest towels ever.

While we reflected on the events of the day and evening, there was a rap on the door; to our surprise and pleasure, champagne was rolled into our room, another gift from our thoughtful children. We slept that night on bunk beds as we had done forty years ago, on our honeymoon trip by rail from New York City to Montreal, Canada — the difference being that there were no damask sheets then.

The luxury train made its way to Paris, passing many small towns and cities on the journey. The train took us to Calais, France, where we boarded a boat operated by the Orient Express to take us across the English Channel. Halfway across the channel, the waters became rough, and some of us had to endure some discomfort. But after the storm cleared, we could see the White Cliffs of Dover; the cliffs were truly white, beautiful, and evoked from the travelers onboard a deep emotional response.

Everyone seemed to remember the much beloved song from World War II, and one could actually imagine bluebirds flying over the cliffs as the song described so long ago. We arrived safely in Dover, and were transferred to another Orient Express train; although not quite as luxurious, it was elegant, and took us to our first destination — London, England.

LONDON, ENGLAND

London, England, holds so many interests; however, we had decided not to overextend ourselves trying to see everything. Our anniversary dinner was in the dining room of a hotel recommended by the concierge, and we were pleased with his recommendation. We attended the London theater performance of *Cats*. Bernie was thrilled; for me, while the music was excellent, I detest cats; for this reason, I had not consented to see the New York performance.

We allowed time on this visit to see the crown jewels in the Tower of London; we had to endure a long wait in line, but the jewels were worth it. We shopped Regent Street without dining, and spent hours in Harrods Department Store. There were several nerve-wracking bomb scares by the IRA during our stay there — one in the underground subway system, and the other in Harrods; fortunately, we missed both of them. We visited Westminster Abbey, watched the changing of the guards at Buckingham Palace, and strolled along the Thames River; we had quite a relaxed visit.

AMSTERDAM, NETHERLANDS

We flew to Amsterdam after our week in London. Although vastly different from London, we found the Netherlands interesting and its canals intriguing. We had reservations at the Zandvoort Hotel, in Zandvoort, located on the North Sea — a hotel with many amenities, but a distance from Amsterdam. We went into Amsterdam almost every day, and noticed the lifestyle of the younger set was somewhat Bohemian, as reflected by their clothing, hairstyles and recreational enjoyment. In comparison, we saw many college students entering schools and theatres and using libraries, so they appeared culturally sound. We enjoyed the students as they, too, went through the Rijksmuseum, Amsterdam's most famous museum, while we all enjoyed the paintings of Rembrandt.

Most interesting were the canals and waterways, although they made driving very difficult for a tourist. In fact, we had our car booted because we did not understand the parking system and we overextended our allotted time. After we found the police and motor agent to pay the fine for our ignorance, it took hours for the police to release our car. They ignored all I had to say about visiting their country and courtesy.

The following day, we drove to Amsterdam and took a boat ride on the harbor, which was pleasant and relaxing; actually, we saw much of the city from the water. A visit to the Flower Market was a tour we were glad we decided to take, as the market was filled with the most gorgeous flowers of every conceivable color and species, and the beauty seemed to comfort our souls. The Netherlands exports more bulbs than any other country in the world; tulips, of course, were the largest export, and gladiolas and hyacinths were second and third. The gardens completed our sightseeing day.

The following day, we had the sobering experience of visiting the house of Anne Frank, a small row house facing a canal. We could feel the misery and confinement of this young girl and her family. I felt stifled on our short visit, and marveled at the Frank family's ability to survive such an ordeal.

On this same day's excursion, we stumbled onto the red light district of Amsterdam. We were strolling along looking at a map, when we saw a crowd of people ahead of us looking up at a window, which was open and available for all to see. When we reached the site, I was frozen in place when I, too, looked up in the windows and saw the exhibition of women being gawked by passersby. Women adorned only in colorful corsets were gyrating and beckoning for the tourists to enter. It was quite a startling public display.

This was a presidential election year in the United States; thus, we had absentee ballots mailed to us in Amsterdam so we could exercise our privilege. We were so excited when the ballots arrived and quickly filled them out and returned them to the nearest post office. Somehow, that process made us feel extremely patriotic.

On long drives, we saw much of the countryside of the Netherlands. As we drove along the back roads, we found very few windmills, and most of those found were electrically driven; I was disappointed. We decided to spend a day in Belgium and drove down to Antwerp, arriving in time for lunch in an outdoor café, and later dinner, before heading back to Zandvoort where we had lodging. We were still amazed that we were able to drive so quickly from one country to another.

FRENCH ALPS

From Amsterdam, we took an overnight train to our next destination, Marseille, France, where we rented a car to drive up the French Alps. The car did not have an automatic choke, and did it give us trouble! For the first hour, we did not understand the problem: we literally crawled up that mountain.

Night was beginning to fall, and we were to check in before dark. The constant stopping was exasperating, difficult, and caused undo delay. We called the resort to notify them that we were on our way; by the time we reached the resort, it was pitch black in those mountains, and we were exhausted, hungry, and disenchanted with the French Alps.

To add to our misery, we were greeted by a disgruntled clerk, annoyed because she had to leave her home to greet us. We had no French francs, nor did she have any to make an exchange for us. Fortunately for us, Bernie met some Americans in the lobby who gladly exchanged some of their French currency to help us with the money situation.

The next day, we were able to have the car checked, as well as secure some francs. Our new-found friends invited us to bring our dinner to their apartment and dine with them that evening. That made for a pleasant evening, but we all decided that there was not enough activity here, as most of the scenic routes in the French Alps had been closed for the season.

The following day, we drove back to Marseille, found a hotel room, and began to use our Europass for the balance of our stay in France. The rail system in Europe is efficient, clean, and reliable. We used the train between Marseille, Cannes, Nice, and Monaco. The Europass allowed unlimited trips, so we enjoyed the French Riviera, the beaches and coastline in Cannes, and Nice. The area is totally beautiful, with opulent designer boutiques frequented by the rich and famous, and well cared-for shorelines, hotels, and restaurants. There were very few people in the area at that time of year; thus, the beaches were vacant and we could appreciate the aesthetics of the landscape. The restaurants and hotels were very accommodating.

I was intrigued by Monaco, mostly because its princess was an American; therefore, we decided to spend a day to explore the small principality. Monaco was very worth the visit: the area was picturesque, with the blue Mediterranean Sea, and a splendid coastline with homes, restaurants, and resorts in the hills. I, of course, wanted to see the palace of Prince Rainier and Princess Grace. The palace is high above the water and is exquisitely beautiful; the flowers and grass that surrounded the building were ornamental and lovely.

The Grimaldi family have been monarchs of this principality for generations, and in the throne room of the palace there was an imposing family portrait of Prince Rainier, Princess Grace, and their three children, dressed totally in casual white attire; it was a superb family portrait. We enjoyed all we surveyed of the French Riviera; it is a beautiful, unique part of the world.

COSTA DEL SOL, SPAIN

From the beautiful French Riviera, we used the Europass to travel to Barcelona, Spain, where we stored some luggage so that our visit to Malaga would be less cumbersome. Malaga is on the Costa Del Sol, or the Spanish Riviera. Not quite as beautiful as the French Riviera, it is, nonetheless, a lovely place to visit; we enjoyed this part of the Mediterranean Sea and the extraordinary coastline. We loved the friendly locals and dined in some of the local restaurants and cafés.

Having found complete relaxation in the neighborhood while strolling, we saw an advertisement of an anticipated sale of crafts and artifacts scheduled for the weekend. No one had to tell me twice; we would be there. We mounted the hilly terrain to see the numerous vendors with a multiplicity of items for sale. I bought one item and called Bernie to pay for it. Immediately after that purchase, I discovered a mask of a female face made of a black skin that I sincerely wanted. When I asked Bernie to pay for this, he discovered he had no wallet. He was wearing casual pants with multiple pockets, and we frantically frisked him up and down. The wallet was gone.

I paid for the mask and we asked directions to the nearest police station. We felt dejected to realize that someone had so quickly picked Bernie's pocket, and most of those pockets had zippers. Needless to say, we spent the remainder of the afternoon trying to explain to the police our predicament. At the Police Station, there was obviously a language barrier; no one understood us, and we understood enough to know that this was an effort in futility. We gave up and left our hotel address, making the unbelievable assumption that the wallet might be returned.

We returned to our apartment and immediately placed a call to our son with the instructions to stop payment on all credit cards. Our son, Carl, promptly informed us that we were in the pickpocket capital of the world. Obviously, that bit of information had escaped us; fortunately, I, too, had an American Express Card and a few Travelers Checks left. At the American Express Office, we obtained enough money to get us through the last week of our trip. I had wanted to visit Torremolinos, but the heart for that vanished with the loss of the wallet.

SWISS ALPS

We left Malaga poorer but wiser, and eager for our next destination, Leysin, Switzerland. We had to return to Barcelona to retrieve our luggage left there, and board a train to Leysin, in the Swiss Alps area.

To our intrigue and amazement when we arrived, we were required to make the balance of the trip on a cog wheel train, up the mountain to the lovely Leysin Park Hotel. What beauty and charm! We were directed to a gracious apartment, simple but inviting in décor, with the most magnificent view of the Alps and a balcony where we could inhale the pure, clear, fresh air surrounding us.

This was heavenly beauty: snowcapped mountains above and lofty puffs of white clouds below our balcony. I remember going on the balcony one morning, raising my hands to God, and thanking Him for allowing me the privilege of visiting this beautiful place, another part of His masterful creation. It was truly a blessing.

On our first evening there, we found it difficult to leave the view to have dinner. However, we went to the dining room and noticed it was not crowded; we even had window seats. Shortly, a large group of tall, muscular, mostly blond men were seated to dine. From the waiter, we learned they were the Swiss National Basketball Team.

As unusual as it was to use a cog wheel train to arrive at the hotel, it was also unusual to learn that we were the only guests in the hotel. The following morning, when we arrived at breakfast, the dining room was empty, so I inquired of the waitress if we were late for breakfast. She replied, "You are the only ones for breakfast." Can you imagine being the only guests in a hotel? Service was more than exceptional for a few days. I recommend this to anyone who can obtain it — what a feeling!

The following day, from that lofty location, we climbed a nearby mountain. The first person we saw was a black woman speaking French rapidly to her small children. We laughed; we had seen few black people on this trip, and here at the top of the mountain, almost out of the world, we see her. We are just everywhere, we happily thought.

There was a well-established small town up the mountain that included a cheese factory. Needless to say, our curiosity was aroused and we requested a demonstration of their cheese-making. In huge wooden vats, they stirred and continued to stir the milk and curd until the cheese was formed; Gruyere is one of the well-known varieties of cheese from Switzerland. The workers, as well as other local people in this area, wore their traditional clothing, and interestingly enough, some school children ate lunch in the cheese factory on a daily basis. The children brought their own lunches, but received a beverage from the establishment. This gave us a little glimpse of their culture.

On the night of the United States election for president, we pulled out a sofa bed in the living room, brought in two dense down comforters from the bedroom, and spent the night eating, tallying votes, and enjoying our election night in a foreign land. We had actually seen a sign inviting any American who wished to meet with other Americans to the recreational area to watch the election results, but we decided to do this alone.

The next day the cog wheel train took us down to a more populous civilization, where we boarded a train to Bern, the beautiful capital of Switzerland. The guide took us on a tour of the old and new city of Bern, and the contrast was interesting. I could not understand the Swiss fascination with bears, especially the bear pit in the center of town. The pit contained many active brown bears. Also, a bear appeared on their city flag, and there was a bear on their coat of arms.

Our guide explained that Bern translates to "bear," named because of the killing of a bear by the Swiss founder.

In the old section of Bern, there were many historic buildings, some with red-tiled roofs and flowing fountains. The old and new sections were connected by spans of bridges over the Aare River. New Bern had museums, botanical gardens, and many international organizations headquartered there, such as the American Red Cross and the United Nations Educational, Scientific, and Cultural Organization (UNESCO). The tour was very informative.

We departed Switzerland for home; our five-week odyssey was over, and we enjoyed all we had seen. The landscapes, the Mediterranean Sea, the coastlines, and the mountains were unbelievably beautiful, and again, we had been enlightened by people and their cultures, and the magnificence of God's creations.

Post Epilogue

We still reside in Moorestown, New Jersey, where Brenda, Mark, and Carl completed high school. We continue to travel within the United States and elsewhere, and have visited Alaska (by sea and land), Portugal, the Netherlands, Ghana, Australia, and New Zealand, and returned to France, Spain, and England. Our most recent trip was to the Greek Isles.

Brenda is now a physician, with a specialty in Obstetrics and Gynecology. Presently she is director of the Residency Program at Advocate Illinois Masonic Hospital in northern Chicago, where she and her family reside. She has studied Spanish to better communicate with some of her patients. Brenda is married to Paul S. Watford, and they are the parents of a fourteen year old son, Everett A. Watford. Travel is still very important to her family, and they have traveled to Kenya, Africa, cruised the Seychelles, visited China, Tahiti, Belize, Australia, New Zealand, the Greek Isles, and other places not visited in her youth.

Mark is now an attorney, having attended Georgetown Law Center, in Washington, D.C. His area of expertise is energy law, particularly in the field of natural gas. He recently accepted a position with the Laclede Group in St. Louis, Missouri, as General Counsel. Mark still has a passion for golf, the game he learned to love while living on Kwajalein. He is married to Vivian Austin Darrell, and they have two children: Elizabeth, age fourteen, and Matthew, age twelve. Travel and people are also important in their lives.

Carl, our youngest son, attended Georgetown University, obtaining a degree in Finance and Computer Science, and obtained an MBA from Monmouth University. While working for Lockheed Martin, he was selected to go to

Tokyo, Japan, as their man in finance. Since he had to interact with the banks, he had to learn the language quickly. He spent five years there, enjoying the work, the people, their discipline, their culture, and the language, which he continues to study.

Carl left Lockheed Martin for a five-year period to work in the sports arena for Disney in Orlando, Florida. However, he recently returned to Lockheed Martin, and is enthused about his future in a new job. Carl is an avid skier, and his greatest amusement was indoor skiing in Japan, but his serious skiing occurred at the site of the Winter Olympics in Japan. He is most proud of his two climbs up Mount Fuji. He has traveled to the Great Wall of China, the Philippines, Bali, Indonesia, the Greek Isles, and many other places not traveled in his youth, especially if skiing occurs there.

We have instilled in all of our children the love of travel, and of knowing and appreciating other cultures. They have seen much of the world, its people, places of interest, and the beauty associated with travel. They have learned that many accommodations are still needed if we are to live in peace and harmony.

Acknowledgments

Dr. Ruth Fisher, a dear friend who edited the book, made suggestions, read and re-read, and was not afraid to tell me "That has to be done over." I love you for that and all your enormous help.

Mrs. Barbara Green, a friend and neighbor, read, reread and critiqued, making many helpful suggestions.

Mrs. Gwen Collins, who read a draft, was extremely excited and encouraged me to get it finished.

Mrs. Saundra Allen, who read, critiqued, and offered many helpful, pertinent suggestions.

Mrs. Rose Holder, my mother, who saved and cherished each letter and postcard received from us during our travels. The collection was an enormous help, as it filled in many details that jogged my memory. Sadly, Mother passed away in December 2005, never truly realizing the contribution she made to this project.

Bernie (Edgar), my husband, who helped to keep my memory in check; who was so proud of me for tackling this project, plus, who was thrilled we could use some of his photographs from our travels for this memoir.

Photograph Credits

The *Tarlang*	Kentron Kwajalein Calendar
Re-entry Missile Measurement	Kentron
Postcard	Unknown
Mr. Leher with Bernie	RCA *Family News*
Bernie's Personnel Collection	

About the Author

Barbara M. Darrell was born in Harrisburg, Pennsylvania, and reared in Brooklyn, New York. New York City remains very close to her heart. She resides in Moorestown, New Jersey with her husband, Bernie (Edgar). She has been active in community causes: Family Service of Burlington County and the Grandparents Program of the Moorestown Elementary Schools. She is an active member of Bethel African Methodist Episcopal Church, Moorestown, New Jersey, with a particular interest in fund raising. Barbara is an alumnae member of the Rancocas Valley Chapter of Links, Incorporated. Her greatest pleasures are reciprocal visits with her children and grandchildren, and her winters on Hilton Head Island, South Carolina.

Chapter 7

FRIENDS and FEELINGS

Amazingly, my new friends on Kwajalein lived very near me in New Jersey. Our husbands worked together at RCA; however, I had no true relationships with the wives until we were six thousand miles from home. Since co-workers on a small island must be nice, we encountered no hardships or difficulties. If our new friends had an agenda, certainly this was no place to display it. We were well received and the RCA wives continue to be friends to this day; the couples have dinner every two months, and many of the wives have lunch on an almost weekly basis. Consequently, our friendships have deepened, from sharing the joys of weddings, births, bar mitzvahs, and anniversaries to sympathizing and grieving when there is an illness or loss of family members.

However, RCA wives were not my only island friends. I had friendships with non-RCA wives, black women who remain connected until this day. Although distance prevents frequent visits, we manage to keep in touch; the bond of friendship is strong and permanent. Addie Johnson, an MIT wife, and Barbara Lyght, a military wife, both arrived on the island after my arrival; they became my connection to my race, and only we could share the frustration and hilarity black women face with their hair especially, in a white world. Interestingly enough, we each chose to handle "the hair situation" differently: Barbara chose to relax her hair and then go to the beauty salon for a wash and set; Addie preferred to complete her entire process herself; I resorted to perms in Honolulu and my assortment of wigs when the perms grew out. Technology has relieved black women of this problem, thank God.

Notwithstanding all these good relationships, one afternoon I heard the paperboy berate my son Mark using the N-word. I jumped up from my nap and ran to the door to see what was taking place. I immediately called the *Hourglass* and told the manager I did not want that boy delivering my paper again. He was fired; his father called me that evening to tell me of the number of Negro friends he had. I did not want his friendship, just his respect. Obviously, his mistake was in not teaching his youngster to respect all people.

Kwajalein life was a unique experience in numerous ways, and only one who has lived there can truly relate to those experiences. Since Kwajalein was a military installation, there was a diverse population from almost every region of the United States on the island, plus people from the Philippines and the Marshalls. Frankly, I had never lived so closely with so many different nationalities before, at least not close enough to become friends, entertain them in my home, and become totally involved in their lives. Basically, the care and love of family was the same, while the foods and religions were different because of different ethnic or geographic backgrounds. Kwajalein represented a multi-ethnic and multi-racial mix that was both interesting and educational.

In our mobile U.S. society, many corporations send employees to various parts of the world to perform given tasks, and that is their main focus — to successfully perform the task. I had never lived so close to so many white Southerners before, and it was good to dispel some of the false beliefs I held. Much to my amazement, most of them were very nice people; even though I realized some were only superficially nice, that is true of populations everywhere.

Since I had been educated in integrated schools and worked with people of many various nationalities, I had learned to get along well with most people, despite their regional, religious, or ethnic differences. However, when one has lived a lifetime of discrimination, one's antennae quickly pick up if a new acquaintance is worthy of friendship, whether he is Northern or Southern. Thus, it does not take long to determine if a person is prejudiced. There were occasional innuendos, to be sure, but nothing I was unable to handle or ignore. The daily injustices suffered in the States prepared me to live anywhere without feeling crushed or dejected. Kwajalein was a Utopia compared to life in the United States. Bernie and I were always open-minded and raised our children to be the same, which allowed them to expect fairness.

Chapter 8

ACTIVITIES and LIVING

Many things kept us busy on Kwajalein, and entertaining was a major component. Fortunately, I was raised by a mother who believed in beautiful table settings and careful food presentations. On Kwajalein, dining became an art form as well as entertainment. If one accepted an invitation, an invitation was owed. It was fun and my recipe collection grew.

One really great entertainment I enjoyed putting on for the ladies on a Saturday afternoon was a "Come as You Are" party. I planned a finger food menu — which we called *puu puus* in Hawaiian — and then called all the ladies about an hour beforehand and requested that they come to my trailer as they were dressed. Everyone came except one lady who thought I was joking. We had such a wonderful afternoon — so relaxed, so much fun — while our husbands worked.

The women on the island gave some outstanding dinner parties; many of them were great cooks and bakers. We still share recipes even today; in fact, there are several Kwajalein cookbooks floating around being used currently. I think my love for hosting dinner parties and luncheons evolved from this experience.

In addition to the entertaining, other great activities abounded. Island living was amazing, nothing tedious or mundane about this existence. One example of this was the full carnival held annually, where Dally Field was converted into a midway with a ferris wheel, merry-go-round, airplane ride, Dunk the Mermaid booth, the Nerve Game, Bingo, a Fish Pond, Coin Toss, and much, much more.